THE CRIMSON TIDE

THE CRIMSON TIDE

ALABAMA FOOTBALL

GEORGE LANGFORD

The Illustrated College Football Series
General Editor: George Vass

Henry Regnery Company • Chicago

Library of Congress Cataloging in Publication Data

Langford, George, 1929 –
    The Crimson Tide.

    1. Alabama.   University — Football.   I.   Title.
GV958.A4L36   796.33'263'0976184   74 – 6899
ISBN 0-8092-8363-8

Photographs courtesy of Citizens Savings Athletic Foundation
and the Alabama Journal Sports Department, Montgomery,
Alabama. Special thanks for Davant collection photographs to
the Southeastern Conference Commissioner's Office.

Published by Henry Regnery Company
114 West Illinois Street, Chicago, Illinois 60610
Manufactured in the United States of America
Library of Congress Catalog Card Number: 74-6899
International Standard Book Number: 0-8092-8363-8

Contents

Section One:
The Coaches

1

Denny's
"Continuous Journey"

Dr. George H, (Mike) Denny bit down hard on his pipe, almost as if he were about to undergo surgery without anesthetic.

The anticipated collision happened and the scholarly-looking gentleman in the blue business suit and wire-rimmed glasses staggered backward slightly. After gathering himself he peered down at the heap of jersey and leather at his feet.

"Sorry, Sir," whispered the brawny student, who bounced to his feet and trotted away, an oval ball tucked under one arm.

Denny peered at the young man and adjusted his glasses. If his face remained stoical, there was a secret smile underneath.

This did not appear to be the proper circumstances for a university president but Denny, who held that position at the University of Alabama, was there for an ultimately academic purpose.

It was an important part of his daily routine to attend football practices because the game filled a significant role in his grand plan. When he became head of the school in 1912 there were only 400 students, four classroom buildings, three dormitories and one fraternity house. Denny felt there was a crying need to get the school moving, to attract students, to build a name, a reputation.

For these reasons—and because he loved the sport—Denny devoted his autumn afternoons to viewing practice from dangerously close quarters. It was almost as if he were inviting accidents.

Zipp Newman, who as sports editor of the *Birmingham News* for half a century covered almost every Alabama football team after Denny's arrival, chuckled at the memory of Dr. Mike's absorbing his daily hematoma.

"Dr. Denny watched every practice and the players were a little bit superstitious," Newman recalled. "They thought if they could knock him down or hit him they would win the next game. He got knocked down a lot . . . but he didn't get injured."

Indeed, if Denny was getting struck before every Alabama victory in the '20s and '30s he was taking a consistent beating. But Denny, as Newman noted, was not getting hurt. Far from it, particularly in an aesthetic sense. Denny was seeing his beloved football team gradually increasing the nation's awareness that there was a University of Alabama. And that was part of the design.

Newman and others who have followed the development of Alabama football give most of the credit to Denny for creating the atmosphere and providing the interest and impetus that enabled a sports dynasty to be conceived.

Until Denny arrived at Alabama, and for several years thereafter, the football was undistinguished. As one historian wrote: "Alabama had been active in Southern football practically since the beginning but never won a championship and never been considered much more

Dr. George H. (Mike) Denny,
President of the University of
Alabama from 1912 to 1937.

Wallace Wade, Alabama
head coach, 1922-1930.

than a second rate power."

That covered the time from its first game in 1892 to 1923 when a virtually unknown assistant coach from Vanderbilt University named Wallace Wade became Alabama's sixteenth head football coach. From that time forward, with the exception of a brief lapse in the 1950s, Alabama's success at the game and its persistent growth have been virtually unparalleled.

It is significant, in fact, how closely the unrelenting annual domination by Alabama football teams has followed the personal motto which Denny adopted when he undertook the task of building the University.

"Success is not a definition," Denny maintained. "It is a constant, continuous journey."

Denny also coined the term "Capstone," which many

Alabama folk use as an affectionate nickname for the University. It developed when Denny, during an early speech, said he wanted to make the University "the capstone of Alabama education." In many subsequent years it also has been the capstone of national football.

"The best break Denny ever got was getting Charlie Bernier from Hampton-Sydney to be the athletic director," Newman maintained. "Denny had known Bernier at Hampton-Sydney. Bernier was the first man who really scouted over the state for players. He found a lot of great ones. In turn, Bernier brought Hank Crisp from Hampton-Sydney in 1921 as an assistant coach to Xen Scott. Dr. Denny, Bernier, Scott and Crisp really got the whole thing started. They deserve credit for building the foundation for Wallace Wade."

Although the teams preceding Alabama's emergence under Wade were not overwhelming, they left behind a storehouse of lore that remains an integral part of its football legacy.

The sport was slow in finding its way from Rutgers, N.J., where it had its beginnings in 1869, to the red clay hills of Alabama. When it finally arrived in Tuscaloosa 23 years later, it came through fateful circumstances.

William G. Little, a 220-pound Alabama school boy, had been sent off to Phillips-Exeter Academy in Andover, Mass., to complete his secondary education with an eye toward entering Yale. While at Phillips-Exeter he encountered the strange new game. It fascinated him and the sport, in turn, was suited for Little because his size made him a particularly valuable lineman.

Several more years might have passed before football was introduced to Alabama, but Little was abruptly called back to his home in Livingston when his oldest brother Jim died. Little trooped back carrying with him his canvas football pants, a ball, cleats, and his fondness for the sport. Instead of Yale, he chose the convenience of Alabama and in the fall of 1892 organized the first team at the University.

Little was named captain. E. B. Beaumont, who had learned about football while attending the University of Pennsylvania, was appointed coach, and the first game was arranged for Friday afternoon, November 11 in Birmingham at Lakeview Park, a baseball field. The opposition was described as "Professor Taylor's Athletics," which consisted of a pickup squad drawn from several high schools. Professor Taylor also was center on the Athletics but that didn't seem to bother the University boys. Alabama won 56-0 and its records treat the game as a regular contest. Others insisted it was a practice in preparation for the real thing the following day against the Birmingham Athletic Club. Sketchy records of the battle with Prof. Taylor's Athletics suggest it featured some spectacular plays including a 30-yard touchdown run by Little (who played guard), a 75-yard gallop by end D. A. Grayson and a 50-yard scoring romp by halfback Dan H. Smith.

Quarterback for Alabama that day was 145-pound Will Walker, who later became a judge in Birmingham. Little went on to serve as a probate judge, fullback William B. Bankhead rose to be speaker of the House of Representatives in Washington, and Bibb Graves, a substitute, twice was elected governor of Alabama.

The players wore padded pants, stockings, tightly laced canvas jackets, and a few owned hockey caps. But for more head protection the players were encouraged to dispense with haircuts. The helmet didn't appear until the early 1900s, along with the jersey, nose guard, and shin guards.

Little and his "Cadets," as they were called, returned to Lakeview Park the following afternoon to play the older and more experienced Birmingham Athletic Club. It was the scene for one of the most spectacular kicks on

Speaker of the House
William B. Bankhead in 1940.

record, a 63-yard drop kick by J. P. Ross of the Athletic Club in the final minutes of the game. Because a field goal counted five points in those days and a touchdown only four, the remarkable boot enabled the Athletic Club to defeat Alabama 5-4. Little had scored the only Alabama touchdown on a guard-around play but Quarterback Walker had missed the conversion. Earlier, Alabama had driven to the "five foot line" where the Athletic Club stopped the march.

Apparently, however, only Ross's kick saved the game from being an artistic flop. A report of the game described it thus: "Both teams resorted almost exclusively to mass plays, using what was commonly referred to as the 'V' or wedge play. Fumbling was frequent."

Alabama really had no excuse for losing, because their coach enjoyed a position of preeminence during the game that no coach since has experienced or surely ever

Jim Ryba,
All-American tackle, 1937.

will. The last line of the story explained that "Coach Beaumont of Alabama was the referee and Walter Winn the umpire. Their decisions met with general satisfaction."

It was almost a month before Alabama played next and again the opposition was the Birmingham Athletic Club. D. A. Grayson ran 65 yards for a 'Bama touchdown and after a fifteen-minute intermission during which "bruises were rubbed, stiff legs limbered up, cuts patched and wind restored," Alabama scored twice more, kicked one two-point conversion, and won 14-0 for Coach Beaumont.

There is some dispute whether the fourth and final game actually belonged to the 1892 season or was an early opener for 1893. It was played on February 22 and marked the beginning of a bitter (and subsequently long-interrupted) series with state rival Auburn. It featured the flying wedge, which Auburn apparently employed with greater effectiveness since the Tigers won 32-22. The most notable aspect of the game was that it attracted more than 5,000 spectators. Football was gaining popularity rapidly in the deep South.

Alabama finished its first season with a 2-2 record. It lost all four games the following season under new Coach Eli Abbott, who was a tackle on the 1892 squad, and was 2-1 in 1894 entering the final game against Auburn. That Thanksgiving day, November 29, produced the first truly significant Alabama victory. Abbott was still the coach and after a year's inactivity had put himself back on the team as a running back. The coach was to be involved in a spectacular play.

Writer Fuzzy Woodruff published *The History of Southern Football* and devoted considerable space to a poetic description of the big event:

"Poor, puny Alabama had lost to Auburn twice the year before and Auburn's machine was far better this year.... A remarkable crowd estimated at 4,000 was at Riverside Park (in Montgomery), an old state fair grounds field that was within a mile dirt track for trotting horses.

"On the far side of the field were the high seated traps and low slung victorias, the fashionable equipages of the day and each conveyance was gay with colors and pretty femininity. The entire student bodies of both schools had made the journey to Montgomery and all the young men wore their hair in the exaggerated chrysanthemum shape that was then the mode.

"Before the game the first charge of using ringers was made. Auburn charged Alabama was to use two players especially imported from the University of North Carolina for the game.

"If so, it was never proven because they didn't play.... Collecting tickets and handling water buckets that day was a fellow named Champ Pickens, who pro-

Carey Cox, All-American center, 1939.

moted Alabama trips to the Pacific Coast 30 years later.

"From the start of the game it was apparent that Auburn, despite its vaunted strength in the line, had nothing that could match the fury of the Alabama forwards. The attack was led by Jim Shelley, the halfback, who repeatedly crashed over Frank Cahalan's tackle to lead an 18-0 victory."

Abbott was the only coach during the first thirteen years to last three consecutive seasons and he departed immediately after the 1895 squad lost all four games. But Abbott, a persistent sort, came back to play end for the 1896 team coached by Otto Wagonhurst that won two of three games. Three years later he played against Alabama for the Tuscaloosa Athletic Club.

Educators, however, were beginning to frown on the violent sport, particularly after the death of Georgia play-

Tom Hupke,
All-American guard, 1933.

er Von Gammon in 1897 in a game against Virginia. Alabama thus was permitted to play just one game in 1897 and did not field a team in 1898. The school yearbook, the *Corolla,* explained it this way:

"In reviewing our past athletic season (1897) we find very little to be proud of. Handicapped by the stringent law of the Trustees which prevented our traveling, we were compelled to play our baseball and football games on the campus."

From the *Corolla,* which summarized the problems of 1898, comes this paragraph:

"We have seen that it is useless to attempt to put out a football team so long as we are compelled to play all of our games on the campus."

In 1899 football resumed. W.A. Martin, who graduated from the University of Virginia, was named coach and his team won three and lost one. Said the *Corolla:*

"Athletics have made a greater advance than in any preceding year. For the past four years our teams have been kept at home like children but this year the guardians of the University have allowed them to visit twice a year in charge of a nurse to keep them from harm. Our football team was very light but nevertheless reflected great credit on our splendid coach, Mr. Martin."

Martin, however, was gone the next season when M. Griffin directed the team to a 2-3 record including a 53-5 loss to Auburn. Naturally he was replaced in 1901 by M. H. Harvey, an Auburn graduate who didn't fare much better (2-1-2 with a 17-0 loss to his alma mater).

Eli Abbott popped up again in 1902 as a volunteer coach along with J. O. Heyworth after a Mr. Sedgwich, who had been appointed coach, abruptly quit. The 1903 *Corolla* emphasized the vacillating coaching situation and the unprofessionalism of the office when it noted: "Both refused to accept any compensation for their services. Mr. Heyworth not only did this because of his love for the game but paid the expenses of the substitutes to the Georgia game in Birmingham."

Two former Yale men, W. B. Blount in 1903 and 1904 and Jack Leavenworth in 1905, were employed to coach but it was not until 1906 that Dr. J. W. H. Pollard, captain of Dartmouth in 1885 and athletic director at Union College in Rochester, N.Y., became what most 'Bama followers considered their first true coach.

"Pollard was a helluva coach," remembered Zipp Newman. "He was the most professional coach Alabama had ever had and the first brought in from the outside with any kind of reputation. Pollard was tricky. He pulled a lot of things. And he was a brilliant man. Auburn accused him of cheating—using ringers—and he may have. Auburn probably used them, too. But that was one of the things that caused the Auburn-Alabama series to be stopped. (It ended after the 1907 game and was not resumed until

1948). If Pollard was lucky, he was paid $2,000 a year."

Pollard designed such plays as having his backs hoist the fullback and fling him over the center. He directed his linemen to join hands much like the Radio City Rockettes and do a sidestep in unison to either side, then break apart. Both maneuvers were quickly outlawed.

Pollard moved up to Washington and Lee after four highly successful seasons at Alabama where he won 21 games, lost only 4, and tied 5. It should be pointed out that even in these early years under the most unstable circumstances, Alabama was winning. From 1892 to 1905 it won 35, lost 32, and tied 2 under nine different coaches. In fact, from 1904 until 1950 Alabama did not experience a single losing season. Pollard got the tradition in high gear and Dorset Vandeventer Graves, who followed Guy S. Lowman in 1911, rattled off four winning seasons before Thomas Kelly, a product of the University of Chicago, took over for three successful years. Football was suspended because of World War I in 1918 but the following year the game really became a serious matter at Alabama. Dr. Denny and a thin little coach named Xen C. Scott saw to that.

2
Wallace Wade

Xen Scott was a popular figure at Alabama. His relaxed manner and engaging personality made him easily likeable. But doubtless it was his success as a football coach that was the real reason for his general acclaim. Had illness not intervened, it is likely Scott would never have left the void that provided Wallace Wade with his opportunity to succeed him.

Scott was the first coach to bring a measure of national prestige to the school when his 1922 team traveled to Philadelphia and upset the University of Pennsylvania before 25,000 fans in Franklin Field 9-7. The victory was a shock to Yankee football followers. But Scott's record should have forewarned them that this "bunch of little ole country boys," as they referred to themselves, would not be easy prey.

Scott, though a tiny man, had played the game at Western Reserve University in Cleveland, Ohio, and had coached at Penn State. He learned to survive more through shrewdness than sinew and it served him well as a coach. He was, perhaps, the first real offensive strategist at Alabama and surely was the first and only sportswriter to coach there. Because the coaching business paid no more in 1919 than it had ten years earlier when Pollard earned about $2,000 a year, Scott moonlighted in the summer writing about thoroughbred racing for a newspaper in Cleveland.

His debut at Alabama in 1919 was sensational. Scott's team won its first five games and did not surrender a point while accumulating 225 during that streak. It lost only to powerful Vanderbilt (16-12) and finished with an 8-1 record. The 1920 club was even better, providing Alabama with its first ten-victory season including the University's first triumph over Vanderbilt 14-7 after five successive losses to the Commodores. Scott employed a variety of confusing shifts and used the forward pass as a major weapon in 1920.

Alabama even had a star under Scott. His name was Riggs Stephenson, who was one of its first triple-threat backs. Stephenson could smash up the middle, sprint outside end, pass, and punt. He was the forerunner of the modern linebacker on defense and played 60 minutes in virtually every game. His play made him one of the first players from the University to be named to the All-Southern team.

But Stephenson's first love was baseball, as it was for two other 'Bama players during that period, Luke and Joe Sewell. All three won jobs playing for the Cleveland Indians. Stephenson, in fourteen seasons as both an infielder and outfielder for the Indians and Chicago Cubs, hit .336. Joe Sewell was a sure-handed shortstop with a .312 batting average over the same period. Luke Sewell was a renowned catcher for 20 years and managed the St. Louis Browns to their only American League pennant in 1944.

Scott profited while these athletes were cavorting

with a football at Tuscaloosa. Joe was a back in 1919 and Luke filled the same position a year later. Scott also had others helping. Charlie Bernier had been appointed athletic director in 1919 with specific instructions from Dr. Denny to produce winners. Bernier did much of the recruiting of athletes for Scott. And in 1921 Bernier lured Hank Crisp to Tuscaloosa as a line coach. Crisp doubled as a talent scout.

It was a winning combination. Scott's teams were wide open, exciting clubs that began to entice followers from throughout the state. Scott put Stephenson in the tail of a modified punt formation offense, shuttled his line, and ran up some huge scores. Where Scott dwelt primarily on the backfield, Crisp was an expert on the fundamentals of line play and his forwards quickly developed a reputation for being among the most devastating and well-drilled in the south.

The critics, however, scoffed at Scott's enviable 18-2 record during his first two seasons at the Capstone and in the words of Zipp Newman told Scott "to go out and get a reputation."

So Scott obliged, scheduling a game with eastern power Pennsylvania in 1922 at Philadelphia—and winning!

Scott's career was beginning to soar at that moment. Few at Alabama had ever heard of Wallace Wade, an assistant coach at Vanderbilt. Alabama fans had a coach and they were happy with the teams that were representing the University. But Scott was dying of cancer and in less than a year Wade would replace him.

The ailing Scott, in fact, secretly submitted his resignation the day before the second game of the season against Oglethorpe on October 7, 1922. It was to take effect at the end of the year. But by October 28 when Alabama traveled to Austin, Texas, and fell to the University of Texas 19-10, Scott had lost 35 pounds. Doctors ad-

Wallace Wade.

vised him not to make the long journey from Austin to Philadelphia but Scott insisted. Bernier was forced to step in and help the rapidly-failing Scott from the bench in that memorable game. Not long afterward Alabama lost the first coach to whom it had genuinely become attached.

Denny's first reaction at the resignation of Scott was to launch a search for the best available replacement. His first choice was Daniel Earle McGugin, the man who from 1904 to 1934 won thirteen Southern championships at Vanderbilt with a record of 200 victories, 56 losses, and 13 ties. McGugin, however, was settled in Nashville and declined the offer. He recommended instead that Denny hire Wade, Vanderbilt's line coach.

Wade already had applied for the head coaching job at the University of Kentucky and had been invited to Lexington for an interview before the athletic board. But

Fred Sington, All-American tackle, 1930.

he became irritated when he was asked to leave the room while the board began a long deliberation over his qualifications.

The taciturn Wade finally exploded. He stormed into the room just as paper ballots confirming him were being tossed into a hat. He had received the unqualified offer from Denny and was not going to tolerate further delay. He told the board:

"I am going to Alabama. And the University of Kentucky will never win a football game from a team of mine."

Wade's teams made the threat a promise kept. Kentucky never beat him in eleven meetings as head at Alabama and Duke.

When Wade arrived at Tuscaloosa he found that Scott, Bernier, and Crisp had done thorough ground work that would enable him to quickly elevate the reputation of southern football to the highest level.

Wade's personality was the opposite of Scott's. He was crusty, blunt, disciplined, stubborn, a perfectionist without equal. They either did it his way or not at all.

At the time of his arrival at Tuscaloosa for his first collegiate head coaching job, the south had produced only two All-American players since the game had been introduced to the area more than 30 years earlier.

When he left Alabama eight years later—allegedly because of differences with Denny—he not only had developed three All-Americans but had taken the first three southern teams to the Rose Bowl. And they returned unbeaten! His clubs had won four Southern Conference championships and compiled a 61-13-3 record. Wade had started a fever for winning at Alabama which would only grow hotter under Frank Thomas and Paul (Bear) Bryant.

Wade was an extremely stubborn man. Yet he was sometimes quick to change. And he was always exploring ways of varying an offense or defense. Some considered him more of a defensive coach because he put such emphasis on that phase as well as the kicking game. But he is given much credit for developing a number of other offensive formations.

Wade's technical genius was only part of the reason for his success. His absolute love of football and a personality that struck fear (and immediate respect) into the hearts of his players also were major factors.

There are several anecdotes, some apocryphal, about Wade's toughness.

Once, in the middle of a game, one of Wade's players told his coach he was too sick to continue playing.

"Sick," stormed Wade. "Boy, get sick on Christmas day, the Fourth of July, get sick any time but don't get sick in the middle of the biggest game on our schedule."

It irritated Wade to hear his players yelp if injured.

He often said: "If yelling 'Oh!' would help, I'd yell 'Oh!' for you."

Wade needed only three years to produce Alabama's first bowl team when he took his 1925 squad across country to the Rose Bowl and what would become the biggest single victory in the school's history.

Alabama was a 2-to-1 underdog on New Year's Day 1926 against the University of Washington, and their brilliant back George (Wildcat) Wilson. The odds seemed pretty accurate at halftime when Washington led 12-0.

But two things happened. Wilson suffered an injury and missed most of the third quarter. And Wade, in what he later considered his finest bit of halftime maneuvering, changed his strategy. On defense, Wade moved to stop the end runs of Wilson by shifting two heavier men to those positions—Guards Ben Ennis and Bruce Jones. Offensively he junked the play using his star Johnny Mack Brown running outside and instead sent Pooley Hubert crashing up the middle.

Alabama scored 20 points in seven minutes of the third quarter and won 20-19.

At the time it was called the Rose Bowl's greatest game, the one that may have saved the classic and the victory that gave southern football its biggest boost. It was the twelfth Rose Bowl and Wade had as much a hand in the triumph as any coach possibly could. He took Alabama to the big bowl twice more before he left, getting a 7-7 tie with favored Stanford the following year and demolishing Washington State 24-0 in 1931, another victory attributed to Wade's genius.

The triumph over Washington State was Alabama's last game under Wade. He had resigned in the spring of 1930 after turning down a five-year contract and accepted the head coaching position at Duke University. Since he had one year left on his previous contract at Alabama, Wade remained to honor it—and took a team that had not

Pooley Hubert, All-American back, 1925.   Wu Winslett, All-American end, 192

been highly regarded in pre-season estimations to the Rose Bowl again.

Many gave Wade credit for one of the great coaching jobs of any era on that New Year's Day 1931. Wade had many motivations that afternoon, not the least of which was to show Dr. Denny and those at Alabama who had criticized him, what they were losing. He also remembered that Washington State had beaten the Brown University team he had played on in the 1916 Rose Bowl. Wade could never rationalize defeats. He remembered them all.

This day Wade devised an unusual piece of strategy. He started his second team, something he had pulled occasionally before.

Wrote a west coast observer:

"The vaunted defense of the Western Champions

University of Alabama varsity, 1930.

crumpled like the walls of Jericho before an amazing pass attack which caught the Northmen flat on their heels. The 'Bammers unleashed a passing and cleverly-masked running offense which the canny Coach Wade kept stored in the cooler all season long. And before it the touted Cougars were just corn pone and 'possum pie. That freckle-necked southern gentleman who coached the Tide won today's game with his noodle, and don't let anybody tell you different. Wade sat out there on the bench and outfigured the lads from the north all afternoon long. First he dispatched his shock troops into the fray at the onset and while his second stringers were holding the fort he analyzed the weaknesses and strengths of the opponent.

"Then, 'midst the roars of approval from the joyful band of Dixie rooters in the stands, he sent in his regulars to win the ball game. And they did just that."

But why was Wade leaving after so much success? It is a question Wade never answered and others have only guessed about.

Zipp Newman, who knew Wade as well as anyone at Alabama, had a theory.

"There were several things that caused him to leave but the main was that he and Denny had a falling out ... originally over the location of the new stadium. Wade wanted the stadium out from Tuscaloosa. Denny wanted it downtown where it is (Denny Stadium was dedicated in 1929)," Newman said.

"I remember the day Wade resigned. He was a little superstitious and he wanted me to come out to his house only on Wednesdays. That Wednesday I went out and he had gotten a letter from Duke indicating they wanted him to become head coach.

"He showed me the letter and asked if I would go see Denny. He called him the 'Old Man'. He wanted to see if the Old Man would let him go to Duke. So I went to the campus and I saw Dr. Denny walking out of his office down the steps. I went up to him and just came right out with it: 'Doctor, are you going to release Wade to go to Duke?'

"Denny had a big pocket watch in his vest and he reached in and pulled it out. He looked down at it and said: 'Zipp, you want to make your first edition don't you?' I said: 'Yes.' Then he said: 'Well, you better get down to the damn telegraph office and write that Wade has been released to take the Duke job.' "

Victories weren't the only dimension Wade gave to the game. He was quick to realize the value of publicity and may have been the first coach to purchase time to broadcast his team's football games. Despite his bluntness, he was a one-man publicity staff. He invited sportswriters from as far away as Nashville and Atlanta to make the trip to the Rose Bowl with his team for the 1926 game, thereby guaranteeing wide southern coverage of Alabama's exploits. Many credited Wade with saving the Rose Bowl itself. Through his connections made earlier while with Brown, he had convinced officials that Alabama would be a good choice for the 1927 game and historians point to that contest as the one that put the bowl on its financial feet and lent it new prestige.

Wade also developed some of the outstanding football players in southern history. At Alabama he coached Johnny Mack Brown, Fred Sington, and Pooley Hubert, all of whom were inducted into the National Football Hall of Fame. Also there were Johnny Cain, Frank Howard, Wu Winslett, Shorty Propst, Herschell Caldwell, Ellis Hagler, J. B. (Ears) Whitworth, Bruce Jones, Bill Buckler and Ben Ennis.

From Duke came such stars as George McAfee, Al DeRogatis, Tony Ruffa, Billy Cox, Fred Crawford, Jack Dunlap, Earle Wentze, Ace Parker, Bob Barnett, Bob Gantt, Elmore Hackney, Dan Hill, Joe Brumamsky, Eric Tipton, Steve Lach, Mike Karmazin, Bill Milner, and Louis Allen.

Wallace Wade gave Alabama football its prestige. And the University was fortunate enough to have two coaches in its future who would enhance it.

Frank Thomas

The spring of 1930 was a particularly beautiful one in Athens, Georgia. It was also to be an especially significant time for a former Notre Dame quarterback, a roommate of the legendary George Gipp who had been drawn to the south to coach football.

But young Frank Thomas had not anticipated the opportunity that would shortly be presented to him. Neither had anyone else with the exception of three people in Tuscaloosa.

Thomas had just settled in Athens as backfield coach for former Notre Dame teammate Harry Mehre at Georgia. He had come to Georgia as an assistant in 1923. Then in 1925 he accepted the head coaching position at the University of Chattanooga where he developed outstanding teams for four years.

But things weren't going well for Mehre at Georgia and in 1929 he had asked Thomas to return and install the Notre Dame offense. Thomas agreed, figuring at last that

Frank Thomas in 1937.

he, his wife Frances and their little daughter Rita had found a home for a few years.

A phone call the following spring, though, would alter not only that plan but the remainder of Frank Thomas' much-too-brief life.

"Frank," said the voice at the other end of the line, "This is Wallace. I want to talk to you. It's important. Meet me at the track meet in Birmingham."

It was the typically terse Wallace Wade and that was the extent of the information supplied Thomas. But it was enough.

"I'll be there," Thomas replied without hesitation.

When Thomas arrived at Birmingham's Legion Field it was raining. He searched out the Alabama football coach and they huddled together under the shelter of the west grandstands.

Wade characteristically got right to the heart of the

matter.

"Frank, I've resigned here as head coach to take the job at Duke. I'm staying through this season. I have recommended you to succeed me at Alabama," Wade said.

Thomas had contemplated many things that Wade might have in mind at this meeting. But being offered the head coaching job at Alabama had been such an inconceivable subject, he had never considered it for a moment.

Thomas was speechless. Wade quickly outlined the proposition as well as the advantages of the position and told Thomas he would be contacted shortly. End of meeting.

For Thomas, it was a stunning proposal. He was only 31 years old and just eight years earlier had played his final season at Notre Dame where he was the starting quarterback for Coach Knute Rockne, playing ahead of Harry Stuhldreher who the following year would be one of the famous Four Horsemen. If accepted, Thomas would be succeeding one of the game's most successful coaches at the University that was bringing football fame to the south.

As in the case of Wade when he arrived at Tuscaloosa, few had any knowledge of Thomas. But Wade realized Thomas' potential and so did Borden Burr, former star football player at Alabama and an influential alumnus. Edwin Camp, a writer for the *Atlanta Journal* who was familiar with Thomas' work at Georgia, also saw the coaching promise in the young man. All three men recommended him immediately to Dr. Denny. They were aware that Thomas had taken a failing athletic program at Chattanooga and immediately turned it around, winning 34, losing only 11, and tying 2 games in four seasons. Thomas also had returned to Georgia, which had won only four games in 1928, outscored the opposition 155 to 97 in 1929 and improved its record to 6-4.

Thomas returned to Athens to await the next phone call and the days dragged by so slowly that he began wondering if Wade was playing some sort of cruel joke. Finally Dr. Denny called in June requesting Thomas to meet with him in the Birmingham office of Borden Burr on Sunday, July 15, 1930.

Dr. Denny promptly informed Thomas he had been hired, a contract was signed and the University president then delivered his cryptic and somewhat famous analysis of a football coach's value.

"Mr. Thomas," Denny began. "Now .hat you have accepted our proposition, I will give you the benefit of my views, based on many years of observation. It is my conviction that material is ninety percent, coaching ability ten percent. I desire further to say that you will be provided with the ninety percent and that you will be held to strict accounting for delivering the remaining ten percent."

The perplexed and slightly shaken Thomas collared Camp as they were leaving Burr's office.

"Those were the hardest and coldest words I ever heard," Thomas told Camp. "Do you reckon his figures are right?"

"I think the proportion was considerably off," Camp replied. "But there is no doubt the good doctor means what he said."

Thomas returned to Athens and that fall helped Mehre coach the Georgia Bulldogs to a 7-2-1 record. Wade, however, was enjoying his finest season ever at Alabama, blasting all nine teams on the schedule, outscoring them 247 to 13, and earning still another trip to the Rose Bowl on New Year's Day to face Washington State.

Wade was leaving Alabama at its football peak, or so it seemed, and it was an unenviable situation for any successor, particularly one so young with virtually no reputation. When Wade's squad climaxed its unbeaten regular season with a 13-0 victory over Georgia in his final game

Johnny (Hurry) Cain,
All-American fullback, 1931.

at Birmingham, the crowd of 28,000 rose and lavished a long ovation on the departing coach. And Thomas had a good view of the entire scene from the visiting team's bench.

What made Thomas' situation even more demanding was the fact that ten of the eleven Alabama starters would be lost through graduation. Only Johnny (Hurry) Cain, the brilliant running back and punter, would be returning.

Wade may have realized part of the predicament facing his replacement. At any rate, he invited Thomas to travel to the West Coast with his squad for the Rose Bowl.

Thomas watched Wade coach perhaps his finest game against Washington State but if he was at all overwhelmed by the situation he was entering, he never displayed it. Ten days later Coach Tommy, as he came to be known, officially took over as Alabama's head coach. He assembled a coaching staff that included Crisp and Harold

Henry Crisp,
Alabama line coach.

(Red) Drew, who had replaced him at Chattanooga. Then Thomas set out to convert the Alabama offense from the single wing that had been so productive for Wade, to the Notre Dame box which Thomas knew so well.

On September 26, 1931, Thomas made his debut as a head coach against undermanned Howard. Leon Long scored three touchdowns, Hillman Holley tallied twice more and 'Bama won easily 42-6.

Despite the depletion of the Rose Bowl squad by graduation, Alabama won nine of its ten games, rolling up 370 points to only 57 for the opposition in Thomas's first year.

But that one defeat—to the University of Tennessee by a decisive 25-0 margin—nagged Thomas. It was a defeat that helped make Alabama's rivalry with Tennessee its most fierce series, along with the intrastate battles with Auburn which would resume many years later.

Tennessee's great Coach Bob Neyland had competed bitterly with Wade and the intensity didn't lessen when Thomas came on the scene.

Their first meeting was a stage for Tennessee's Gene McEver, who simply overpowered the Crimson Tide. McEver ran for two touchdowns and passed for a third in the victory.

The following season Thomas produced another fine team (8-2) with Cain as the star, but again Tennessee triumphed 7-3 in a storied punting duel between Cain and Beattie Feathers in a relentless downpour. Cain punted nineteen times for an average of 48 yards including the decisive one of just twelve yards. Feathers had a 43-yard average on 21 kicks, one of which traveled just eighteen yards.

Late in the contest Feathers boomed a punt to the one-yard line. Cain attempted to kick out of trouble but got a low snap from center and barely managed to get off the twelve-yarder. Three plays later Feathers went off left tackle for eight yards and the game's only touchdown, wiping out 'Bama's 3-0 lead.

Naylor Stone, who wrote Thomas' biography *Coach Tommy of the Crimson Tide* in 1954, observed that even though Thomas had won seventeen games and lost only three in his first two seasons, he could feel the pressure mounting on him to defeat Tennessee in 1933. It seemed no matter how good the record, a victory over Tennessee was necessary to make it acceptable.

If there was one thing the tough little Welshman loved it was a challenge and General Neyland's orange-clad Volunteers represented one of the first order.

Thomas said it would take "a miracle" to win because his best player, Johnny Cain, had been graduated. And the Crimson Tide had to play in Knoxville where Tennessee hadn't lost a game since 1924 to Vanderbilt.

But the miracle came along in the person of Millard

(Dixie) Howell, a true triple-threat back whose running, punting, and passing on October 31, 1933, brought Thomas a tense 12-6 triumph over Tennessee, the biggest of Thomas' short career. During the game Thomas became so excited he put the wrong end of his lighted cigar in his mouth. Later he reflected that his players had gotten such a big laugh out of the incident he felt it had actually helped them relax.

When it was over the exuberant Thomas told his wife:

"Well, we did it. Now I guess I'll have a job for another year and we'll be able to eat for a while at least."

That was an understatement. Thomas had cleared the last hurdle even though his team lost the following week to Fordham, then a national powerhouse, 2-0 before 60,000 in New York's Polo Grounds.

Thomas led Alabama to four Southeastern Conference championships ('33, '34, '37, and '46), one national title and a record (for that period) of four consecutive major bowls from 1942 through 1946 (with time out one season when no team was fielded because of the war). In fifteen seasons he had a record of 115 victories, 24 losses, and 7 ties and he was elected to both the National and the Helms Football Halls of Fame.

His most competitive adversary paid what was perhaps the finest tribute to Thomas. General Neyland once grumbled:

"That little bastard is the smartest damn coach I ever coached against. If he needed to do something he did it real quick."

Thomas had a sixth sense when it came to judging the capabilities of athletes. That asset plus his quick mind, his ability to devise strategy, and his willingness to devote long hours to the job combined to make him a Hall of Fame coach.

Coach Tommy also had his eccentricities. He seldom

ever answered his mail. It was left to gather on his desk until it was swept aside to make room for another delivery. He had side ventures in politics, stumping around the county for candidates he endorsed. He also had an automobile dealership and sold real estate. He was famous, or infamous, for his reluctance to part with his earnings. Yet he was a tireless fund-raiser for the March of Dimes and the Crippled Childrens' Hospital in Birmingham. And he had time to help students other than football players. Once such a student was interested in a broadcasting career and Thomas enabled him to get a start in the business. The young man's name was Mel Allen, who later became a national sports broadcaster and the voice of the New York Yankees.

Thomas' first victory over Tennessee in 1933 was an indication that he was now ready to match the exploits of Wade. And he wasted no time getting to that goal in 1934. Thomas had the talented players to produce an exceptional team that year and he was keenly aware of it. His left end was Don Hutson. Paul (Bear) Bryant was the right end. At one tackle was Bill Lee. Tarzan White and Charlie Marr played the guards and in the backfield were Howell, Riley Smith, Jim Angelich, and Joe Demyanovich. Howell, Hutson and Lee would be All-Americans in 1934. Smith received the honor in 1935 and White in 1936.

The Crimson Tide began rather haltingly, beating Howard only 24-0. Sewanee fell the following week 35-6 with Thomas using his reserves freely. Mississippi State was an easy 41-0 victim and again Thomas pulled his regulars early anticipating the impending showdown with Tennessee the following week.

Birmingham was the scene of battle this time and the first quarter was a tense, scoreless affair. But the Tide was moving early in the second period, Howell tossing 33 yards to Hutson setting up Alabama's first touchdown and a 6-0 lead. But Tennessee rebounded with a touchdown

Dixie Howell, All-American back, 1934.

Tarzan White,
All-American guard, 1936.

drive that included a penalty against Alabama for slugging. The referee said the offender was right end Bryant, who was ejected from the game. Hutson, however, scored on an end-around in the third period and Alabama twice stopped Tennessee drives deep in its own territory and won 13-6.

"Now," Thomas told his squad, "you can go all the way."

They did.

Georgia was beaten 26-6, Kentucky bowed 34-14, Clemson and Georgia Tech each was drubbed 40-0 and the Crimson Tide came down to the final game against Vanderbilt realizing that a possible Rose Bowl bid awaited if it won. That day Dixie Howell, playing his final game on Legion Field, gained 318 yards rushing and returning

Don Hutson, All-American end, 1934.

punts. Alabama romped 34-0.

Now the Tide waited for word from the West Coast. Minnesota, which was also in the running for the Rose Bowl invitation, had maintained its perfect record by winning that day and the Alabama players asked Thomas what were their chances.

Thomas wasn't sure what to tell them because he thought he should already have received some notification.

When Thomas returned to his hotel there was a message that Los Angeles had called. Alabama had been invited to play Stanford. West Coast fans, however, felt they were short-changed. They considered Minnesota the stronger club and Alabama was ridiculed from the day they arrived in Pasadena with chants of "We want Minnesota."

Thomas loved the put-down talk. It was a great psychological weapon. Physically he worked the Tide relentlessly.

On the day of the game Thomas was a bundle of nerves. He considered this the game that would "make me or break me." And he recalled: "I didn't have a single hot line to deliver like 'From yonder pyramids, forty centuries are beholding you.' But I was thinking that beyond the Rockies lies a lot of railroad track, and if Stanford licks us it will be a long, sad ride back to Tuscaloosa."

Thus Thomas simply reminded his charges how hard they had worked toward this day and concluded: "Now go out there and do it."

Stanford Fullback Bobby Grayson made those words appear awfully empty in the first quarter when he plunged through for a touchdown. But the Crimson Tide rolled back behind the brilliant Howell-to-Hutson connection which accounted for 24 points in Alabama's ultimate 29-13 triumph. And Coach Tommy was "made."

Dr. Denny was so impressed with the triumph that he rewarded Thomas with a new five-year contract and Alabama football was launched into a new phase which would never see a losing season under Coach Tommy in his 12 remaining seasons. Only once—in his final year in 1946—would the Tide lose as many as four games.

Graduation again stripped the Tide of talent in 1935 but Thomas mustered a 6-2-1 record including a victory over Tennessee. The following year he was denied a perfect season only by a scoreless deadlock with the difficult Volunteers. Thomas added two new assistants to his staff that year and one of them was Bryant. Along with Crisp, Drew, Tilden Campbell, and Joe Dildy it represented one of the strongest staffs in college football. Thomas was never afraid to surround himself with capable helpers.

Thomas also had some talented players that year,

Joe Kilgrow,
All-American halfback, 1937.

enough—he felt—to reach the Rose Bowl again. As in 1934, the bid seemed to ride on the outcome of the final contest on Thanksgiving Day against Vanderbilt in Birmingham and it was a thriller. The Commodores took an early 6-0 lead and held it until late in the third quarter when Joe Riley's passing asserted itself. Riley passed to Ben McLeod for the tying score and Joe Kilgrow kicked the extra point. In the final period Kilgrow grabbed a touchdown pass from Riley and the Tide had a 14-6 victory.

Thomas fully expected an invitation from Pasadena or at least a bid from the Sugar Bowl. But the West Coast opted for Coach Jock Sutherland's University of Pittsburgh Panthers with such stars as Bill Daddio, Frank Patrick and Bob LaRue. The selection rankled Thomas because the Panthers had lost to Duquesne 7-0 and had been tied by Fordham. The Sugar Bowl chose Santa Clara

Bill Lee, All-American tackle, 1934.   Vaughn Mancha, All-American center, 1945

and Louisiana State, the Orange Bowl tabbed Duquesne and Mississippi State, and the Cotton Bowl picked Texas Christian and Marquette.

"Can you imagine going unbeaten with only one tie and not getting a bowl bid?" Thomas fumed.

But Thomas used the bowl rejection to his advantage in 1937, spurring his club to a perfect 9-0 record and the Southeastern Conference championship. This time the Rose Bowl could not ignore Thomas. In some respects, though, he wished they had overlooked him because California dealt the fumbling Tide its first setback in five trips to Pasadena, 13-0.

In 1938 the Tide lost only once but it was a 13-0 decision to Tennessee and losses to the Vols never made it a good season. The following year, without a first-rate quarterback, Alabama slipped to a 5-3-1 record and even a 7-2 mark in 1940 would not silence Coach Tommy's growing army of critics. The Tide had lost three in a row to Tennessee and the alumni were restless.

"A few more years like that will make an old man out of your husband," Thomas told his wife. "But this should be a good season (1941). If we don't win, there'll be something wrong."

Alabama was deep in running backs and Thomas used them all. The Tide rebounded with an 8-2 record including an all-important 9-2 triumph over Tennessee. There was also a tingling, last-minute 19-14 victory over Tulane that was a tribute to Thomas' courage as a coach. He called for a quick kick late in the game with 'Bama trailing and it set up the winning touchdown.

Thomas had silenced his critics and displayed his strength as a man and coach. The Tide received its first of four consecutive bowl invitations that year, a bid from the Cotton Bowl. A year later (7-3) the Orange Bowl beckoned. World War II intervened in 1943 and no team was fielded but the youthful 1944 squad went to the Sugar Bowl. It was Thomas' beloved "War Babies," the squad he most admired, which matured and carved a perfect 9-0 record in 1945 and finally got Alabama its long-sought confrontation with Southern California in its last Rose Bowl appearance.

But the gradual effects of a heart condition and high blood pressure were beginning to eat away at Coach Tommy. His moods rode a roller coaster from day to day, being combative and explosive one day and uncharacteristically quiet and easy-going the next. Despite his condition he led the Tide to their finest hour, a 34-14 thrashing of Southern Cal, the Trojans' first loss in the Rose Bowl. Thomas, however, was beginning to make concessions to his illness, admitting that "I don't believe I could have held up all season if my boys hadn't given me such a lift with their performances."

Early in 1946 doctors advised Thomas to curtail his pace drastically. He was ordered not to stand. He had to direct practices from a trailer. It would be his last and "least enjoyable" season as head coach. When he wasn't at practice he was in bed, and his condition worsened to the point that before the Tennessee game in mid-season Dr. Raymond Paty, now president of the University, asked him to resign for his own good. Thomas refused, but losses to Tennessee, Georgia, and Louisiana State finally convinced him to step aside. Thomas was appointed athletic director but he was constantly in and out of hospitals and finally gave up the job in 1951. On May 10, 1954, Thomas died.

4

Red Drew

Harold (Red) Drew was a good coach. No one should have been disappointed with a man whose football teams compiled 55 victories, lost only 29 games and tied seven in eight seasons. But Drew's timing was all wrong. He was asked to step in and continue the pace set by two Hall of Fame coaches, Wade and Thomas. Not even his record of taking the Crimson Tide to the Sugar, and Cotton, Bowls or the Tide's smashing of Syracuse in the 1953 Orange Bowl seemed to satisfy alumni who had been spoiled by near perfection.

Drew had been an assistant to Thomas for 12 years before leaving to try his hand as head coach at the University of Mississippi. Thomas had urged his good friend to take the position. But when Thomas became ill and obviously could no longer continue, Drew was the first mentioned as a successor.

Thomas told the athletic board he would be able to continue as athletic director but wanted Drew to be the

Harold D. (Red) Drew in 1948.

new head coach if he could be convinced to leave Mississippi.

There was no persuasion required. Drew quickly accepted the invitation and in his first season led the Tide to an 8-2 record including a 10-0 triumph over Tennessee and a date in the Sugar Bowl. The visit to New Orleans resulted in a 27-7 defeat by Texas and made many people forget Drew's accomplishments in his first year as head coach. Drew's next two seasons were mediocre by the Alabama gauge (6-4-1 and 6-3-1), but in 1950 Drew's outfit fashioned a 9-2 record, losing only to Tennessee and Vanderbilt.

The alumni howled the following year (1951) when Alabama suffered its first losing season since 1904, but Drew battled back with a 10-2 worksheet in 1952 that included the 61-6 Orange Bowl triumph over Syracuse. A year later he won his only Southeastern Conference title with a 6-2-3 mark. The Tide lost the Cotton Bowl to Rice 28-6 in the famous Tommy Lewis contest. Lewis came off the bench to tackle Rice's Dicky Moegle, who was winging toward a touchdown.

Nothing seemed to go right thereafter for Drew. He had not beaten Tennessee since his first season and when his 1954 team finished as his second loser (4-5-2) in four years he became Alabama's first coach in modern times who was forced to resign by alumni pressure.

Almost any other college would have been pleased with the work of the rugged man from Maine who had played at Bates College and who, as an assistant to Thomas, had developed star ends such as Hutson, Bryant, and Holt Rast. He had contributed considerably to the victorious Thomas years through his recruiting, and during his head coaching administration he had seen the resumption of the Auburn series in 1948. Drew's teams had beaten the state rival five times in seven games, and the Auburn contests were beginning to surpass the Tennessee tests in alumni emphasis.

But Drew lost to lightly-regarded Mississippi Southern twice in succession his final two seasons and his 1954 squad was shut out in four of its last five games. A 27-0 victory over Tennessee was ruined by a 28-0 beating by Auburn in the final game.

The alumni wanted another Wade, another Thomas. It would be three more years, the bleakest in Alabama football history, before a man of such caliber would be found. They succeeded only in forcing out a talented and much-loved coach, ironically in the same year that his close friend, Frank Thomas, died.

Drew stayed on as an assistant professor of physical education and track coach and he was too big a man and too much attached to Alabama to gloat over the disaster that befell his successor, J. B. (Ears) Whitworth during the next three years.

The capsule summation of Whitworth's stay might best be illustrated by his handling of one player — Bart Starr.

Zipp Newman recalled the situation:

"Drew had said a couple of years earlier that Starr was going to be one of the best passers Alabama ever had. A lot of people realized he had some potential although I don't think anybody suspected he would be as good a pro as he was. But Whitworth didn't use him much. One day I said: 'Whit, you've got a helluva prospect here for a passer.'

"Whit said: 'Well, he's got to fit into my system.'

"I said: 'Well, Whit, that's an unusual statement. Coaches tell me they try to fit their system around the boy instead of the other way.'

" 'That's not the way I coach,' Whit said."

Whitworth left Starr and most of the other seniors on the bench in his first season as head coach and Alabama didn't win a game.

Things never worked from the beginning for Whitworth. Alabama scored just six points in its first four games under him and the new coach never seemed able to gain control of the situation. The Crimson Tide, in fact, never came close to winning in 1955, the smallest spread being Vanderbilt's 21-6 triumph in the second game of the season.

Whitworth didn't win his first until the fifth game of his second year when the Crimson Tide edged Mississippi State 13-12. Alabama defeated Tulane 13-7 later that year and Whitworth got two victories in 1956, 14-13 over Georgia and 29-2 over Mississippi Southern.

Alabama had won just four of 30 games under Whitworth and when his contract expired on December 1, 1957, the University announced it would not be renewed. Two days later in Houston, Texas, a press conference was held in the Shamrock Hotel and a tall, ambling man whose face was as creased as his gray suit was named as Whitworth's replacement.

5

Bear Bryant

Bear Bryant was one helluva football end. Rough and tough as hell. But Hutson got all the publicity ... Bryant beat Tennessee on one leg in 1935 ...

What has made Bryant such a successful coach? That man has more damn energy than any damn man I ever saw in my life. It just flows out of him ... He's one of those determined people ... determined to do something ... I don't think he was too damn good a student at Alabama but his desire, what desire!

—Zipp Newman, February 1974.

A pair of shoes in Moro Bottoms, Arkansas, in 1926 was just about as important a piece of property as a boy could own.

Nobody had more than one pair. A boy wore his shoes for plowing, for driving a team of mules into Fordyce (six or seven miles away) to school, and he polished

Paul (Bear) Bryant.

them up as bright as he could for going to Sunday school and church.

A kid wouldn't think of letting someone nail pegs onto the bottoms of those precious shoes—no kid except 13-year-old Paul Bryant.

When young Bryant let Mr. Clark nail on those cleats, it was the first tangible sign of "angry ambition which drove Paul all the way, which would not let him be still, which insisted that only first place would do."

Bryant had never heard of a football until that day. Living so far from Fordyce High School, he never had time for anything—until the Bryants moved to town—except driving the mules to school and back for his sisters, loading up the wagon with produce from Papa Monroe Bryant's farm, and climbing in beside his mother and ringing the bell, peddling vegetables from house to house.

"I hated that peddling worst of all," Bryant recalled. "And ringing that bell. . ."

So the day when he just happened to be walking past the Fordyce High School football field was the day he found a way, found something better than peddling, something into which he could pour all of his burning ambitions.

"I was a big ole gawky kid," Bryant remembered. "And the coach came over and asked me if I'd like to play awhile.

"I told him, 'Yes, I guess I do,' but I didn't even know what they were playing. I think I must have been covering punts that first day because the coach just pointed me down the field and told me to run down there where that fellow catches the ball and hit him."

Bryant laughed softly when he recalled how he went "clacking around" everywhere after Mr. Clark put on the cleats because they wouldn't come off.

"Papa told me I couldn't play. I slipped off and played anyway and my Mama and Papa never saw me play football. They were deeply religious and didn't believe in a lot of things like movies and football.

"Even after I was coaching, my Mama would come to our house on the day of a game but she would stay at the house and take care of things."

Bryant's most fabled athletic achievement—if you could call it athletic—occurred the following year, most people believe, when Paul was 14. And it didn't happen on a football field. It was the time Bryant earned his nickname, one he doesn't care for and which friends never use. It was the time he climbed into a ring before a packed house in Fordyce's Lyric Theater and, for an amount of money (no one is sure how much or if Bryant ever received it), "rassled" a bear.

"It was a mangy, little old bear," one of Bryant's friends recalled. "It's a disgrace for a man to get famous over tangling with something like that. He ought to be ashamed."

Another friend of the family insisted the bear was 10 feet tall and the meanest bear he had ever seen.

Anyway, there was young Paul, wearing a pair of old overalls, ready to tackle the bear. Some say after a couple of minutes of tussling, the bear's muzzle came off and the owner got frightened and stopped the show. Others say the owner tore off the muzzle because he saw the bear was going to cost him money.

Bryant would rather remember about football and the first time he rode in an elevator when Fordyce went to Little Rock for a game; when he first went to Dallas for an all-star game and left the stadium at halftime and rode a street car back to the hotel so he could listen to his favorite team, Alabama, play in the Rose Bowl.

"I always wanted to play for Alabama, ever since I can remember," Bryant said. "There was this fellow in Pine Bluff—Jimmy Harland—who had sort of adopted Alabama as his team and he influenced me a lot."

After his senior year at Fordyce, Bryant got a job working on highways for the state of Arkansas, and that is where Coach Hank Crisp found him.

"He asked me if I wanted to play for Alabama and I told him: 'Just let me get my satchel' and we left right then for Tuscaloosa."

There he roomed with All-American Don Hutson and played the end opposite Hutson. There he quickly decided that coaching was everything he wanted to do in life and it was there he met and married a campus beauty, Mary Harmon Black. It was also there that Frank Thomas spotted the embryo of something special, something that prompted Thomas, in 1942, to call Bryant "potentially the greatest coach in America."

Thomas was never more right about anything in his life. Bryant started his coaching career as an assistant under Thomas, then moved to Vanderbilt to assist Red Sanders in 1940 before enlisting in the Navy during World War II. He accepted the head coaching job at Maryland in 1945 after the war and in 1946 moved to Kentucky in the same capacity.

He took the Wildcats to four bowl games in eight seasons, won the Southeastern Conference title and compiled a 60-23-5 overall record. Next was a four-year term as head coach at Texas A. & M. The Aggies were 1-9 in his first year, 1954, but were unbeaten and the Southwest Conference champions just two years later. Finally he came back to Alabama in 1958 and a career that had been outstanding quickly became unparalleled.

Entering the 1974 season, Bryant's Crimson Tide had captured 140 victories in sixteen seasons, lost only 21 games and tied seven. He had taken the Tide to fifteen consecutive bowls. Alabama won seven Southeastern Conference titles under Bryant, three national championships, and twelve times in sixteen seasons finished in the top 10 of the Associated Press final college football

Bear Bryant watches a practice, 1973.

ratings.

He had produced 27 All-Americans at Alabama, won the national Coach of the Year award in 1961 and 1971, and was voted Coach of the Decade by the American Football Coaches Association in the 1960s. His teams had won 231 games in 29 years as a head coach, an average of eight victories a season, and 20 of those teams went to bowls. Eight of the teams won at least ten games. Bryant ranks third in total victories among all coaches in history, trailing only Amos Alonzo Stagg and Glenn (Pop) Warner, both of whom had many more years of service.

Bryant's success has been so distinctive and his standing at the University so immense that the head coach and athletic director was able to make a personal gift of $100,-000 to the University in 1973 to fund academic scholarships. If such an action is unprecedented, so is the man.

In Alabama, a visitor is quickly aware of Bryant's unique standing. He inspires grammar school boys to dream, teenagers to trim their hair and grown men to stiffen in his presence, remove their hats and ask in reverent tones for his autograph.

Men are moved to print postcards, design posters—even erect billboards—proclaiming "We Believe". The name even commands awe in places where nothing has been sacred since Jefferson Davis.

Bryant, in essence, has become a reluctant deity in Alabama. He would like to be just a football coach but his worshipers demand much more. At one time they wanted him to be governor, senator, or even President.

The real zealots, though, argued: "Why should he step down?" He had reached the summit among his people. He runs the most successful college football team in the nation in an area where football is religion, love, and law.

Outsiders, dissenters are ignored in Alabama just as resolutely as Bryant is adored. There are signs with a caricature of Bryant striding across Mobile Bay captioned: "O ye of little faith."

Bryant's supposed ability to walk on water has plagued him for years and after Alabama's close loss to Notre Dame in the contest for the 1973 national championship in the Sugar Bowl, an Alabama fan was asked what happened to his coach's supreme power.

The fan never hesitated in his reply:

"Aw, the Bear was just out walking his ducks and he got hit by a motor boat."

The worship embarrasses Bryant, but he is a pragmatic man.

"They make me look ridiculous," he once drawled in his graveled monotone, "but the fans get a kick out of it, so what does it matter? The jokes are silly, but they don't offend me—anything to sell tickets."

Bryant had a plan for handling this deification. He had a plan for success, too, and a plan in case of failure, which landed in the wastebasket. He always had a plan to use when a practice session was good, bad, or mediocre. He always had a plan for his reaction if his team won by a big score, a close margin, or if it lost or tied. There was a plan, too, if his team played poorly and won or played well and lost. Bryant had a plan for everything.

Physically, Bryant, who was 60 years old in 1974, might recall a likeness of Lincoln. His long, ambling legs, jutting chin, lean, handsome features, and seemingly inch-deep creases drawn from his eyes and mouth could send one scurrying to examine tintypes.

Bryant is phlegmatic when he discusses himself. During an interview he rarely assumes more than two positions in his chair. He sits in a slouch with his legs extended—making them appear even longer—with his elbow resting on the chair arm and his other arm draped across the back corner of the chair. Often the only movement is the constant cigarette to and from his lips.

A smile is usually reserved for a subject other than himself.

Like many people in the athletic fraternity, he feels the need to unwind often, yet he has religious convictions that apparently go very deep. He senses his position of power and seems to feel an obligation to give much of himself to the public.

His players, former players, and assistant coaches, almost to a man, unabashedly love him.

"I don't care where I was or what I was doing," a member of the 1966 team once said, "If I heard that Coach Bryant was in trouble or needed me, I would drop everything and go to him. He is the greatest man I have ever known and I owe him everything."

It is difficult to mention Bryant's name anywhere in the South without stirring emotions.

He has enemies, jealous contemporaries, and for many years was in an uncomfortable position wedged in a vise of prejudice and racial uncertainty where his word was not the ultimate. Many of the racial problems were eased in the early 70s when the football team became integrated. The young man who helped lead the improvement was John Mitchell, who transferred from Eastern Arizona Junior College and became Alabama's first black All-American as a defensive end in 1972 and became the first black to join the football staff.

Bryant's most difficult hurdle, however, was not integration of a deep South university but a challenge to his honesty contained in a *Saturday Evening Post* article in March of 1963. It accused Bryant and Wally Butts, then athletic director at Georgia, of conspiring to rig a game and of betting large sums on the outcome. Butts allegedly had given Bryant information about his Georgia team prior to their 1962 meeting, which Alabama won 35-0. An Atlanta insurance man, George Burnett, claimed he had eavesdropped on a telephone conversation between Butts and Bryant. The result was a sensational article entitled: "The Story of a College Football Fix" which immediately commanded front page headlines all over the country.

Bryant was already suing the *Post* for $500,000 over an article entitled "College Football is Going Berserk." It was based on an incident in the 1961 Alabama-Georgia Tech game. Alabama led 10-0 and time was running out. Tech halfback Chick Granning received a punt and was tackled hard by linebacker Darwin Holt, who whacked Granning with a forearm in the process. Granning was seriously injured.

Atlanta writer Furman Bisher charged Holt and Bryant with "dirty football" in the *Post* article. Bisher also did research on the "fix" story.

Bryant's suits eventually amounted to $10,500,000 and the legal harangue went on for a long period. It was the most difficult time in Bryant's life.

He was besieged, however, with friends and character witnesses, none of whom were needed in court. The case was settled out of court for $300,000, and Bryant and Butts were exonerated. Butts won a record-breaking libel judgment that originally called for $3,060,000, but it was later reduced to $460,000.

A trainer who had been with Bryant at Texas A.&M. recalled an incident that convinced many that the Alabama coach could never have been involved in such a sordid affair.

"That first season he coached at Texas A.&M. was the only losing season Coach Bryant has had (1-9) and the next year we started out against U.C.L.A. which was ranked Number One and lost, 21-0," the trainer said.

"Louisiana State was next and it looked like we'd never win another game. But some veterinarian from Louisiana sneaked up in a tower of a dormitory overlooking the L.S.U. practice field the week before the game and took movies of their workouts.

"When this fella brought the films in and offered 'em to our assistant coaches they were tickled to death. They took 'em in to Coach Bryant and he told them: 'I don't want 'em. If we have to win a ball game like that I'd rather lose.' "

The story is documented and the veterinarian even came forth to testify in Bryant's behalf. The final score is also documented. It reads Texas A.&M. 28, L.S.U. 0.

"Bear Bryant is no saint," cautioned one regular in the Stafford Hotel in Tuscaloosa where Bryant regularly stops for coffee.

"Nope," agreed another old-timer. "Saints can't walk on water."

From the Stafford Hotel dining room where Nettie and Jerri serve coffee, one can see the downtown lights shimmering off the surface of the swimming pool in the early morning darkness.

Sometime between 5:30 and 6 A.M. Bryant strides in and finds a seat in a booth.

There, alone, Alabama's No. 1 citizen will quietly open the paper, check the financial and sports pages, sip his coffee and have a couple of cigarettes. He occasionally jokes with the waitresses or one of the customers although there isn't much business so early.

Bryant might laugh about his golf game or shake his head about the time he used to have for hunting and fishing, but he never tarries at the Stafford because there will be more than a dozen assistant coaches waiting in his office for a 7 A.M. meeting.

That was the ritual when he set his most brisk pace in the 1960s.

In the 60s it was about a mile from the Stafford—located three blocks from the center of the Tuscaloosa business district—to Bryant's old offices in the athletic department building which has been replaced by a new field house with modern facilities.

His old workshop was indistinguishable from that of any other college football coach, but wherever Bryant works it becomes a laboratory in which he formulates plans for championships. His staff meetings, according to one assistant, "sometimes last so long you feel like your bottom will fall off."

Bryant's staff is probably the largest of any football team in the nation—college or professional. And from such staffs have come more college head coaches than can be easily tabulated—Bill Battle at Tennessee, Steve Sloan at Vanderbilt, Jerry Claiborne at Maryland, Jimmy Sharpe at Virginia Tech, and Pat Dye at East Carolina, to name only a few.

It is large because Bryant likes specialization and because he feels it is important to give his players as much individual instruction as possible.

The staff is young and ambitious. Bryant, like Thomas, has never been afraid to surround himself with talent. Actually it is this theory of having talented assistants which many maintain is the reason for Bryant's success.

Bryant has delegated more and more of the duties as years go by, but in the 60s he oversaw practice from a tower on the field. If a practice pleased him, the bullhorn remained silent all afternoon. If he spotted a flaw, the bullhorn boomed, usually in a low, steady key. There are fines for profanity for players, assistants, and Bryant.

The assistants are charged with running the acutely organized, precisely timed practices.

"One of the big differences in Coach Bryant and most other coaches today," one assistant coach observed, "is that he plans for every phase—offense, defense, kickoffs, returns, punts. I know a lot of successful coaches like Darrell Royal at Texas who concentrate only on offense and let their assistants handle the rest.

"But Coach Bryant instills great confidence in the coaches and the players because we all know there won't be anything overlooked."

The assistant illustrated the devotion to detail by revealing minute items ordered by Bryant in preparation for the 1967 Sugar Bowl game against Nebraska.

"We knew Nebraska had a left-footed kicker and they used a different brand-name football than we used on offense," the assistant said. "So Coach Bryant brought in a former Alabama player who was a left-footed kicker and he punted to our safety men so they could get used to the reverse spin. And our defense practiced the whole time against a unit using the Nebraska ball."

Bryant claims Alabama practices less than any other team in the country. But there is never a second wasted and, for every minute of practice, hours have gone into the planning.

During many seasons, Bryant's teams have not worn pads in practice after the third or fourth game. Quickness drills are stressed. Through thorough study, an Alabama player knows every move his opponent is likely to make in each situation the next Saturday afternoon.

A boy is never shunted to the side at a Bryant practice. ("I'll never give up on a player regardless of his ability as long as he never gives up on himself. In time he will develop."). The Bear has a rule: "If they stay, they'll play."

Staying, of course, often hasn't been easy. Many players have found in practice they were not willing to pay Bryant's price for success. Many also admit it was the biggest mistake of their lives when they quit a Bryant team.

"When Coach Bryant first came here in 1958, there were 75 freshmen who came out for football," said Jim Sharpe, who was an assistant under Bryant later and one of the 75 then. "He told us to stick with him and that in four years we would be national champions.

"Sixteen of us stuck with him, and after we came back to beat Georgia Tech in 1960, we began to realize that he was right—we could be No. 1," Sharpe said.

Bryant's prediction became a reality. In 1961 he had his first national football champion at Alabama and a new dynasty was born.

But it wasn't easy for the university to lure him back home. He had some definite opinions about coaching for one's alma mater.

Smokey Harper, a trainer for almost all of Bryant's teams, recalled how Alabama finally attracted the Bear after years of fruitless attempts.

"He never thought it was a good idea for someone to coach at his own school. He had seen so many other coaches who went back to their alma maters have trouble," Smokey said.

"Alabama just kept worrying him to come. They

were determined to get him. Finally they told him they were going to discontinue football if he didn't come and I think that was the clincher.

"I remember Mel Allen was in Texas to televise a game just before Alabama made that threat and, being an old Alabama boy, he was asking around as to how they could get him.

"I told him coach is a very sentimental person and that they'd be making a mistake to try to buy him. If they wanted him they would have to appeal to his sentiment. If you talk money, you won't get him."

Smokey was right. Bryant could have all the black-eyed peas in Alabama and a $10 bill for every one of them but he asked for no more money than the University deans were making because "it wouldn't be right to take more."

Steve Sloan, who quarterbacked under Bryant and later became head coach at Vanderbilt, calls Bryant "the most honest man I've ever known."

Bryant likes to call himself a "big ole country boy," which is not really true. Like all exceptional men, he is a complex figure.

He is sentimental and at the same time hard. He is meticulous and scientific, spends hours devising exhaustive plans for every conceivable event, yet he is superstitious.

And football isn't his only arena. Politics has been associated with Bryant in Alabama ever since his close friendship with Ryan DeGraffenried, a Democratic candidate for governor in 1966 who was killed in a plane crash before the primary election.

After DeGraffenried's death, many wealthy and powerful Alabama citizens tried desperately to persuade Bryant—described by one friend as a "wild-eyed liberal when compared with George Wallace"—to become a candidate.

Steve Sloan,
All-American quarterback, 1965.

Bryant deliberated but chose not to run. A newspaperman and close friend said one of the reasons he refused was because of the defeat of Bud Wilkinson, former head football coach at Oklahoma, who lost in a bid to become a senator.

"Wilkinson was always greatly admired by Paul," the friend said, "and he didn't want to lose like Bud did."

In the late 60s there were rumors that Bryant would run for Senator from Alabama. He denied them. "I'm having more fun coachin' than I've ever had. It's the only thing I've ever wanted to do and the only thing I know how to do," he answered.

Bryant chose to demonstrate his convictions through means other than political. The first integrated gathering of any size in Alabama occurred in 1963 when evangelist Billy Graham conducted a "Crusade for Christ" in Birmingham's Legion Field, scene of many Bryant triumphs.

Lee Roy Jordan, All-American
center/linebacker, 1961 and 1962.

As a newspaper editor described the scene, the tension in Birmingham was electric. People feared the racial hatred and bitterness would turn the meeting into a holocaust.

"We almost expected a bomb to go off under the stage," the editor said.

Bryant, in silent endorsement of the meeting and its significance, sat on the stage through the entire program and no incidents occurred. Some people feel Bryant's presence prevented the expected trouble.

Bryant attempted to recruit a black football player as early as 1950 at Kentucky, four years before the historic Supreme Court decision to integrate all schools. He failed on that occasion and admitted he never tried to bring a black athlete to the University of Alabama until the late 1960s. He maintained that he was unable to schedule some of the better northern and western football teams because of the segregation problem. Finally, however, in 1971 Bryant succeeded and by 1973 at least a half dozen Crimson· Tide regulars were blacks including All-American Linebacker Woodrow Lowe and the team's leading runner, Wilbur Jackson.

After the 1967 Sugar Bowl, a black member of the Nebraska football team sought out one of the Alabama stars as he was leaving the field and clasped his hand.

"You know," began the Nebraska player, "I found the reason for your team's greatness. It's your oneness.

"I've never seen a team that has it like yours. We've played a lot of teams in the last three years, but I only saw that oneness when we played you."

The oneness is the end product of the Bryant process. It is a process which sets Bryant, as a coach, apart from others.

The ingredients for his process are culled from those used by every football coach in the land, although there are few who have the ability to blend them successfully into a workable solution.

This is Bryant's special talent. This is the intangible that prompted Frank Thomas to predict his greatness two decades before it was realized.

Bryant will gladly tell any coach the ingredients. The hitch is finding the crucible, which prompts a hardened professional linebacker such as Lee Roy Jordan, a former Bryant pupil, to advise his teammates:

"If coach Bryant orders hamburgers, you order hamburgers. If he wears a green shirt and a purple tie, you wear a green shirt and a purple tie because Coach Bryant is always right."

Bryant quit making trips to recruit high school players in the mid-1960s but he vividly recalled one of the last ones he made in 1965 to Mobile in an attempt to lure one of the state's top prospects.

"I spent three hours talking with that boy and he

talked about everything in the world except football and winning. He asked me a lot of questions, but he didn't ask one about how we were going to win. The only question he asked me is how long we practice.

"I told him: 'Son, I don't know. It might take six or seven hours a day, just whatever it takes to make you a winner.' I said I would like to do it in an hour and 20 minutes but it might take six or seven hours a day for him, and I meant it. Football and winning didn't mean enough to him."

This episode points out much of the Bryant philosophy. Players, coaches, trainers must be "winners"—a term Bryant admits he can't define but can only feel.

"What better way is there to build character, to instill pride than to win?" Bryant asked.

A successful coach is the one who can attain the most from the average player because, as Bryant reasons, most football players are average. A coach must be able to recognize a winning attitude in both assistants and players and also be able to develop such an attitude, Bryant maintained. A coach must be thoroughly organized and, as Bryant puts it, "mentally tough."

"A head coach, in order to achieve the proper atmosphere, must take the attitude that anything that is not good is 'I'. Suppose I'm complaining because we didn't have good material. I know I have to have it. 'I' did a poor job because 'I' didn't get it.

"We go out and lose a football game—it happens to us. I read where people say mistakes beat us. But it wasn't mistakes that beat us. It was me. 'I' beat us because it's my responsibility to train them over and over until they don't make those mistakes.

"In winning, that 'we' takes in a lot of things and there's enough there for everybody but no one actually is rewarded as much in various ways as the head coach. If he is not a guy who is 'I' when everything goes bad, I don't believe he'll ever be a consistent winner."

There is no doubt he is successful. He is perhaps *the* most successful football coach. He has lived his own credo that maintains:

"Winning isn't everything. But it beats anything that comes in second."

Section Two:
The Players

The Men Who First Brought Fame to Tuscaloosa

During the early years of football at the Capstone it was the individual player rather than the modest accomplishments of the teams that drew attention and caused excitement about the sport.

The principal names were Auxford Burks, an exceptional athlete who inspired his fans to poetry; W. T. (Bully) Van de Graaff, a bruising tackle who could also carry the ball, kick, and was Alabama's first All-American in 1915; Center C. C. Countess, who was selected to the All-Southern team in 1908; baseball star Derrill Pratt who captained the 1909 squad; Eli Abbott, who served the team in almost every capacity from player to coach; Riggs Stephenson, who would also make his name in professional baseball as did brothers Joe and Luke Sewell.

They were the forerunners of the great players developed in the Wallace Wade era of the 1920s such as All-Americans Pooley Hubert, Wu Winslett, Tony Holm,

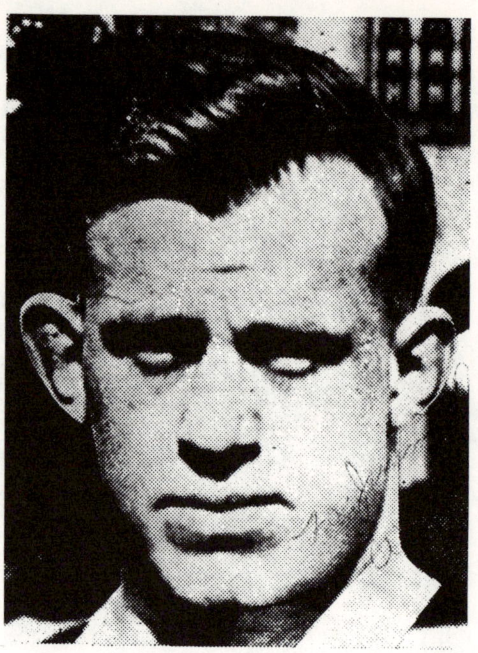

Fred Sington plus Johnny Mack Brown, Bill Buckler, Bruce Jones, Grant Gillis, Al Clemens, Fred Pickhard, Herschel Caldwell, Emile (Red) Barnes, Gordon Holmes, Monk Campbell, John Henry (Flash) Suther and Johnny (Hurry) Cain, whose successful teams were remembered as vividly as their singular achievements.

Burks was the early legend, the first truly exceptional football player at Alabama. His early clippings testify to his unique abilities on the football field.

Here is an account of his exploits by Fuzzy Woodruff in his three-volume *History of Southern Football,* which covered the period from 1890 to 1928:

"In 1902 Auburn defeated Alabama 23 to 6 but the game introduced to southern football one of its most scintillating figures when Alabama trotted out a substitute halfback named Auxford Burks, a freshman, late in the game.

"... Burks, tall, rangy, powerful...with the most baffling knee action imaginable ... played four years for mediocre teams ... but Alabama football, from its resumption in 1900, grew steadily primarily because of Burks, who led the upset of Auburn (scoring two touchdowns) in 1903.

"... In the 1903 loss to Georgia Tech 12-5, Burks was unstoppable, but fumbles by his teammates stopped Alabama at the goal line. Late in the game Burks finally broke loose for a 45-yard touchdown run but collapsed after the play and had to be carried from the field exhausted."

After running wild against Auburn, the *Birmingham Age-Herald* wrote that "no player has carried the ball so successfully as Burks" and Auburn Coach John W. Heisman, for whom collegiate football's ultimate trophy was named, called Burks "the best running back the south has ever produced."

Burks, who later became a prominent physician in Tuscaloosa, moved his followers to verse. Several poems were published, one of which said:

Greatly to prosper and proudly to grow,
While every hill and glen
Sends our shout back again,
B. Auxford Burks! Alabama! Ho! Ho!
Long shall old Auburn, with groans and with
    madness,
Remember our halfback who played them so fast;
Long shall Sewanee, with wonder and sadness,
Remember our onslaught of November last.
Though this season ends his fight,
Long shall the Auburnite
Think of Burks' tackling with fear and with woe,
Victory upon victory then,
Echoes his praise again.
B. Auxford Burks! Alabama! Ho! Ho!

There was one other earlier performer of a similar caliber. Eli Abbott played tackle on the first Alabama team in 1892, coached the team the next three years, and returned to the field as a running back in 1894, and as an end in 1896.

Borden Burr one of the Capstone's staunchest alumni judged him "the best of all times ... he was loose-jointed. . .piston, high-stepping ... brains and brawn; as hard to stop as a jeep." But there were few around to see Abbott and fewer still who bothered to remember because the teams he coached won only three and lost nine in that first decade of football at Tuscaloosa.

Abbott came back on a voluntary basis to help coach in 1902 when 'Bama finished with a 4-4 record. For many years, however, he also found good football players whom he influenced to enroll at Alabama, including Riley Smith, the All-Southeastern Conference quarterback of the mid-30s.

Bully Van de Graaff was another performer who attracted crowds. A native of Tuscaloosa (for whom the city's airport was later named), the giant youngster had never played football when he enrolled at the Capstone. But Coach D.V. Graves convinced him to try the sport, realizing the value of such an immense athlete in the rugged game.

The year was 1912 and Van de Graaff was a delightful surprise. Not only was he big but he was quick, strong, and a powerful runner who Zipp Newman noted could "knock out tacklers with high-stepping knee action."

By 1915 he was judged the best tackle in the country and was the Tide's main weapon. He ran the "tackle-around play" with devastating results. Van de Graaff, whose brothers Hargrave and Adrian also played at Alabama, was agressive, loved to hit, and was an excellent punter and place kicker. He played every position, includ-

Bill Buckler, All-American guard, 1926.

ing passer, and once threw a 60-yard touchdown to Riggs Stephenson against Georgia Tech. He left Alabama and graduated from West Point in 1916 where his football was curtailed by injuries.

In his final season for the Tide, Van de Graaff narrowly missed a pair of 55-yard field goal attempts which hit the crossbar, and in a game against Mississippi College he kicked four field goals of 45, 40 and 30 yards twice. He had two touchdown runs of more than 50 yards in a victory over Owenton; kicked three field goals in the 16-0 decision over Tulane and played his most satisfying game in the 23-10 upset of Sewanee. That day he accounted for 17 points including a touchdown run of 65 yards with an intercepted pass. Amazingly, over his career he averaged more than 50 yards per punt, scored 12 touchdowns, kicked 15 field goals and converted 45 extra points for a total of 162 points. That wasn't bad for a tackle.

Johnny Mack Brown.

When Coach Wade arrived in 1923 so did the parade of stars. An• All-Alabama team selected over the period covering the first 38 years was dominated by players from the Wade teams:

Alabama's Best from 1892 to 1929

Back	Auxford Burks
Back	Pooley Hubert
Back	Johnny Mack Brown
Back	Riggs Stephenson
End	Wu Winslett
End	Al Clemens
Tackle	Bully Van de Graaff
Tackle	Fred Sington
Guard	Bill Buckler
Guard	Bruce Jones
Center	Clyde (Shorty) Propst

Hubert, a quarterback who could pass, run, and was excellent on defense, was selected to the 1925 All-American team and a year later Winslett won the same honor. Fullback Tony Holm also made it in 1929. Then in 1930 both Sington and John Suther earned All-American recognition.

Voted to the All-Southern Conference team during the 20s were Holm, Sington, Tackle Fred Pickhard (the Rose Bowl star), Halfbacks Emile Barnes, Herschel Caldwell, Brown, Hubert, Grant Gillis, and Stephenson plus Guard Buckler, Center Gordon Holmes, Quarterbacks Grant Gillis and Clemens.

Sington was generally acknowledged as the finest lineman of his day. He weighed 230 pounds his senior year in 1930 but was hardly the typical, lumbering lineman. He was quick, intelligent, and often was able to outrace much smaller players, particularly on punt coverage.

Hubert was recruited as a tackle but was switched to quarterback by assistant coach Hank Crisp who observed his speed and power. (Crisp later called him "the best player I ever coached.") There he became the first in the long line of truly great Alabama quarterbacks and became one of the eight men from Tuscaloosa to be enshrined in the National Football Hall of Fame.

Hubert weighed 190 pounds and was a devastating linebacker on defense, usually playing every minute of a game. His finest hour came when Alabama beat Georgia Tech 7-0 in Atlanta on October 24, 1925. That afternoon he was called the greatest defensive back ever to play on Grant Field. He had 23 tackles, three of them stopping Tech drives deep in Alabama territory, and threw the key block that flattened two Tech tacklers and enabled Johnny Mack Brown to take a punt 55 yards for the game's only touchdown. He also led the comeback victory over Washington in the '26 Rose Bowl.

When Hubert graduated after the 1925 season, Wu

Winslett brilliantly took over much of the passing duties. He led the 19-7 victory over Vanderbilt by throwing touchdown passes of eight and 36 yards to Caldwell. A week later his 36-yard touchdown pass to Archie Taylor sent the Tide off to a 26-7 victory over the Mississippi A. & M. Maroons.

Winslett was the dominant factor in Alabama's 21-0 upset of Georgia Tech in Atlanta the following week. He found Melvin Vines with a seven-yard touchdown pass, hit Taylor on a 35-yard score and threw a 44-yard scoring strike to Tolbert Brown. Against Kentucky he ran for both scores in a 14-0 triumph and in the final game that clinched another Rose Bowl visit, Winslett scored once and passed to Taylor for another touchdown to lead the 33-6 victory over Georgia.

During his tenure at Alabama (1924 through 1926), the Crimson Tide lost only once, won three Southern titles and two national championships. During the season when he was named All-American (1926), not one first down was made around his left defensive end position.

Johnny Mack Brown made the All-Southern selections in 1924 and 1925 but was never quite able to gain All-American honors even though his abilities were near legendary.

After the 1926 Rose Bowl, Head Linesman George Varnell commented:

"Brown has the sweetest pair of feet I have ever seen. The way he managed to elude Washington tacklers in his long runs was marvelous. He has a weaving, elusive style of play that was beautiful to watch."

Washington's star George Wilson said that Brown "was about the fastest man in a football suit I have ever bumped up against."

In the Rose Bowl, Brown scored on a 61-yard pass from Grant Gillis and a 38-yard toss from Hubert, gained 76 yards rushing and made such an impression in

Southern California that less than one year later he was embarked on a long and rewarding acting career in Hollywood. His first movie in 1926 was *Coquette* opposite Mary Pickford.

Sington was regarded as the finest collegiate lineman in the country in 1930, so good in fact that he attracted a remarkable amount of publicity which is never an easy accomplishment for the usually obscure "men in the trenches." The song "Football Freddie," written by Rudy Vallee, was dedicated to Sington.

The Howell, Hutson, Gilmer Years

7

Alabama turned out so many outstanding football players in the 1930s it was hard to select even two teams of All-Stars. But one effort came up with this combination:

Back	Riley Smith
Back	Millard (Dixie) Howell
Back	Johnny (Hurry) Cain
Back	Joe Kilgrow
End	Don Hutson
End	Paul (Bear) Bryant
Tackle	Bill Lee
Tackle	James Ryba
Guard	Tarzan White
Guard	Leroy Monsky
Center	Carey Cox

Cain, Howell, and Hutson all were named to the National Football Hall of Fame in addition to being All-Americans. Cox, Monsky, Ryba, Kilgrow, White, and Lee

Harry Gilmer,
All-American back, 1945.

Leroy Monsky,
All-American guard, 1937.

were also All-Americans as was guard Tom Hupke.

Other outstanding players of the era included guard Charlie Marr, tackle James Whatley, end Erwin (Tut) Warren, back Charles Holm, center Francis Kavanaugh, end Perron Shoemaker, back Vic Bradford and tackle Fred Davis.

The most storied combination of the period was the Howell-to-Hutson passing combine.

Howell stood 5-feet-10 and weighed just 164 pounds, but he developed quickly as a brilliant punter and runner and worked long hours to improve his passing.

In 1933 Howell had an 89-yard punt return against Tennessee, an 86-yard return against Georgia Tech, and an 83-yard scamper with a punt versus Kentucky. He also had an 80-yard interception return against Vanderbilt.

The 1935 Rose Bowl, of course, was one of his major

triumphs. He completed 9 of 12 passes for 160 yards, rushed for 79 yards including a 67-yard touchdown run, returned four kicks for 74 yards and punted six times for a 43.8 average to lead the 29-13 victory over Stanford. He was called the greatest triple-threat of all Alabama backs.

Hutson, like Howell, had a slight build when he came to Alabama. In fact, Hutson did not make his high school football team until his senior year because he was so frail. He entered the University on a partial baseball scholarship but Assistant Coach Red Drew found that Hutson could run the 100 yards in 9.8 seconds and had a smooth, effortless stride. That made the football coach interested.

Still Hutson was slow to develop and did very little in his freshman, sophomore, and first half of his junior year on the gridiron. But during that time he gained 25 pounds up to 185, grew to a height of 6-feet-1 and the extra practice on pass catching began to pay dividends.

Hutson had caught only three passes in 1932 for 30 yards and had just four receptions in 1933 for 48 yards but in the last part of '34 he grabbed 19 for 326 yards and three touchdowns.

His elusiveness came from his remarkable change-of-pace running style and uncanny instinct for the ball. His timing was nearly always perfect. He was an excellent runner in the open field, and he was equipped with large, sure hands.

In the 1935 Rose Bowl against Stanford he was double-teamed by Bobby Grayson and Bones Hamilton, two of the Stanford stars, yet caught six passes for 165 yards and two touchdowns including bombs of 59 and 54 yards.

One of the primary reasons for the success in the 30s was the outstanding succession of linemen. Thomas called Leroy Monsky "the smartest and best guard I ever coached," and called Bill Lee the "best tackle I ever had."

Monsky, a 185-pound guard, was also named the best blocker in the S.E.C. and on defense was one of the main reasons the Tide surrendered only 20 points in 1937.

Other outstanding linemen included Tom Hupke, the first All-American guard from Alabama, 210-pound guard Tarzan White, who later became a professional wrestler, 190-pound tackle Jim Ryba, and center Carey Cox.

There were only five Alabama All-Americans in the 1940s but one of them ranked among the most exciting in the history of the university. He was Harry Gilmer, the jump-pass artist. The other stars were center Vaughn Mancha, tackle Don Whitmire, center Joe Domnanovich and end Holt Rast.

But Gilmer was the unquestioned leader of the time. Grantland Rice was completely taken by the teenage passing whiz and wrote in the *New York Sun* on October 25, 1945:

"Harry Gilmer, barely 19 years old, weighs 158 pounds and he has no such speed as either Blanchard or Davis can show. And yet I saw him pass and run Alabama into 26 points against Duke last winter while tackling all over the field. This fall he threw three touchdown passes against a strong L.S.U. team to carry Alabama into a 26-7 victory over the team that wrecked Georgia, plus Trippi, last Saturday. He then passed and ran Tennessee dizzy to win by 25 to 7.

"Gilmer has already proved himself to be one of the best passers of all time. I'd rank him as the greatest passer in football today, college or professional. But the most amazing part of this 158-pound kid is that he is one of the best all-over-the-field tacklers you'll see in many years, that he is a fine ballcarrier who is not only elusive but who can hold his feet with a 190-pound back. Also, that he is one of the most accurate kickers in the game today. How often do you see a star passer, a fine ballcarrier and a good kicker starring in a defensive role?

"Gilmer's main ingredients are poise, timing and skill. The Alabama star has thin shoulders, a rather thin chest; but he also has a pair of powerful legs and two big,

Don Whitmire,
All-American tackle, 1942.

strong hands . . . he is also as durable as hickory . . . the kid
is as cold as an iceberg. Frank Thomas tells me that no
breaks of the game ever upset him in the least.

" 'I've never seen anyone,' Thomas says, 'who knows
better exactly what to do under all conditions. He can
whip a bullet pass as Baugh does or give you a 50-yard
arm throw of the Luckman type. And he rarely misses his
target. If he ever made a single bad or wild pass I never
saw it . . .'

"Gilmer isn't the only football player Frank Thomas
has on his squad. Big Mancha, one of the best centers in
football, heads a strong, fast charging line. Tew and
Hodges are two hard-running backs. This is the best team
Alabama has sent into action in some years, and Alabama
has more than her share of winning games and winning
years."

Gilmer headed the 1940s team of 'Bama All-Stars

which read this way:

Back	Harry Gilmer
Back	Jimmy Nelson
Back	Lowell Tew
Back	Bill Cadenhead
End	Holt Rast
End	Rebel Steiner
Tackle	Don Whitmire
Tackle	Tom Whitley
Guard	John Wozniak
Guard	Ed Holdnak
Center	Joe Domnanovich

In his collegiate career Gilmer carried 394 times for 1,673 yards, attempted 412 passes and completed 219, suffering only 22 interceptions. Through the air he had 2,894 yards and 26 touchdowns. In 1945 he set a percentage completion record of 65 percent that included 13 touchdowns.

His talents weren't confined to passing. He had a 95-yard run against Kentucky in 1945, a 95-yard kickoff return in the 1944 Louisiana State contest and also a 92-yard punt return in the 1947 L.S.U. game. He returned a punt 80 yards against Georgia in 1947 and in the 1945 Sugar Bowl completed 8 of 8 passes. He rushed for 116 yards in the 1946 Rose Bowl and threw a 24-yard touchdown pass.

"I doubt," said Tennessee's Bob Neyland, "if football has ever seen Gilmer's equal."

Said Frank Thomas:

"I coached Howell and he was the best until Gilmer came along. That was in 1944 and I said then he was the best. I think people are beginning to believe me."

When Gilmer left he was replaced by Ed Salem, a 5-foot-10, 187-pound halfback who would become Alabama's only All-American in the 1950s.

Ed Salem,
All-American halfback, 1950.

The All-50s squad was composed of both defensive and offensive performers since the two-platoon system came into practice during the period:

Back	Ed Salem
Back	Bobby Marlow
Back	Corky Tharp
Back	Cecil Ingram
End	Red Lutz
End	Nick Germanos
Tackle	Sid Youngleman
Tackle	Travis Hunt
Guard	Jerry Watford
Guard	Mike Mizerany
Center	Pat O'Sullivan

Salem, who later went on to own a chain of restaurants in Birmingham and Tuscaloosa, provided the only bright spot for the Crimson Tide during their fall from prosperity. He led Alabama with 879 yards passing in 1950, averaged 15 yards returning punts and scored eight touchdowns.

The previous year Salem was fifth in the S.E.C. in total offense with 558 yards passing, completing 40 of 75 passes for seven touchdowns including a 77-yard bomb that defeated Georgia.

A Tradition of Quarterbacks

Ever since Pooley Hubert first tugged on a Crimson jersey in 1922, the University of Alabama has been known as a cradle for quarterbacks and great passers. The list is long and includes names such as Howell, Gilmer, Salem, Starr, Trammell, Namath, Sloan, Stabler, and Hunter. Most of them graduated to greatness in the professional ranks, proving their exceptional abilities beyond argument.

The recent wave of superb quarterbacks began in the mid-1950s with Bart Starr, although Starr achieved his reputation as a pro with the Green Bay Packers, not in the Alabama uniform. It was Starr's misfortune to arrive at Alabama when the great football depression was hitting. Through a series of circumstances and the change in head coaches from Red Drew to Ears Whitworth, Starr enjoyed relatively little playing time and once admitted "on the whole I left there with a kind of bitter feeling."

As a matter of fact, Starr regarded it as the most

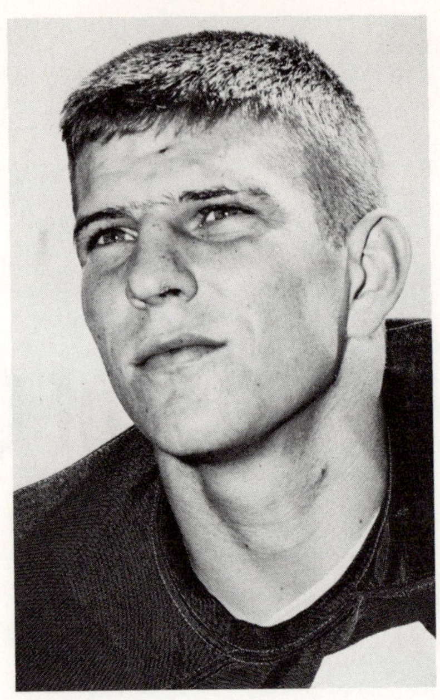

Pat Trammell,
All-American quarterback, 1961.

depressing period in his life because he had always set one goal for himself—to play professional football—and no pro team would be interested in a quarterback who sat on the bench his senior year for a team that lost ten consecutive games.

Coaching had not been Starr's entire problem. Just prior to the start of practice in his junior year he felt something snap in his back while punting. The condition gradually grew worse. Three times that year he was in traction in a hospital and played very little.

When Whitworth replaced Drew the following year the new coach wanted to start a rebuilding program and thus ignored most of the seniors while concentrating on the underclassmen who had a future at Alabama. Starr had been the starting quarterback as a sophomore after playing more than half the time his freshman year. First

Joe Namath, All-American quarterback, 1964.

the back injury then Whitworth's decision seemed to end all his hopes for a chance at the pros.

But on the seventeenth round of the 1956 draft the Green Bay Packers did what Starr didn't dare expect would happen. They drafted him—the 199th player chosen. He later found out that the Packers had drafted him only because of a recommendation from Johnny Dee, who then was the basketball coach at Alabama.

Joe Namath, the day after Alabama's defeat in the 1965 Orange Bowl, signed with the New York Jets for the biggest package ever given a football player to that date, $400,000. His mother, Rose, said her son was worth twice that amount for what he accomplished for the fledgling American Football League despite playing on two bad knees and she was probably correct. He was chosen to the All-time All-A.F.L. squad picked by the Pro Football Hall of Fame. He was the A.F.L. Rookie of the Year in 1965, became the only passer in pro history to surpass 4,000 yards in one season with 4,007 in 1967. He led the Jets to the Super Bowl upset over Baltimore in the 1968 season and was the league's M.V.P. and M.V.P. of the Super Bowl.

The path to this exposure and fame began when Howard Schnellenberger, then an assistant coach at Alabama, came to visit Namath in Beaver Falls, Pennsylvania, in 1960. Schnellenberger, despite opposition from Joe's father, convinced young Namath to enroll at Alabama.

Namath's talent and penchant for headline-making was such that in 1964, although playing only three full games and parts of several others, he was chosen the All-American quarterback.

His collegiate career from 1962 to 1964 was interrupted repeatedly by various knee injuries. Nevertheless he rewrote the Alabama passing book. He completed 203 of 374 passes (a 54 percent completion average) for 2,713 yards and 25 touchdowns. He also gained 563 yards net rushing in three seasons. He scored 94 points and set up 19 other touchdowns either by passing or running.

In 1965, Bryant called the Pennsylvanian "the greatest athlete I've ever coached," even though Namath was suspended by Bryant for the final regular season game in 1963 and the 1964 Sugar Bowl for violating training. Neither Namath nor Bryant ever said what rule was violated but Namath's mother once told a reporter her son had "done nothing except miss the curfew."

Namath came back in 1964 and Bryant credited his leadership both on and off the field as one of the primary factors in the Crimson Tide's surge to the National Championship.

"I've always admired Joe for taking his punishment

like a man when I had to suspend him," Bryant said. "His comeback proved he's a credit to Alabama.

"I never had a gut check like the one I had when I had to fire him," Bryant admitted.

Pat Trammell could not pass with the authority or accuracy of Namath or Scott Hunter, or scramble like Kenny Stabler, but he had a special winning quality about him that endeared him to Alabama.

Zipp Newman said that of all the great Alabama quarterbacks since 1950, his choice would be Trammell because "he always did whatever it took to win."

Trammell was one of the first football players recruited by Bryant for Alabama and he was the one who led the Tide's football fortunes from the darkness of the 50s to the national title in 1961.

"Pat wasn't fancy or anything," said Bryant. "But I'll take him in the clutch when the ball game's on the line."

Trammell quarterbacked Bryant's first Alabama bowl team in the 1959 Liberty Bowl. The next year he led the Tide to an 8-1-2 record including a 3-3 tie with Texas in the Bluebonnet Bowl.

Then in 1961 he was at the controls when the Crimson rolled to ten consecutive victories and a 10-3 conquest of Arkansas in the 1962 Sugar Bowl. Trammell scooted 12 yards over left tackle for the only touchdown in the first quarter, ensuring the national championship.

Trammell, who was selected the Southeastern Conference's Player of the Year in 1961, broke three Tide passing records in completing 75 of 133 for 1,035 yards and eight touchdowns. He was intercepted only four times.

"Pat wasn't fast but he had stamina and deceptive moves in handling the ball," recalled teammate Mal Moore.

When Namath was suspended for the 1964 Sugar Bowl, Bryant turned to an unknown sophomore to replace

Steve Sloan,
All-American quarterback, 1965.

his star. The young man was Steve Sloan, who showed the poise and savvy to get the Crimson Tide close enough for four field goals and a 12-7 victory over Mississippi on New Year's day in frigid New Orleans.

Two years later in the Orange Bowl against Nebraska, Sloan riddled the Cornhuskers for 518 yards total offense in a 39-28 triumph that provided the Tide with its second national title in a row. Sloan passed to Ray Perkins for two touchdowns enabling Alabama to build up a 24-7 lead at halftime.

In his senior year, Sloan shared some of the quarterback duties with Ken Stabler, a lefty. Together they formed a potent pass-run combination.

Stabler was an exciting scrambler, and when he took over the full-time quarterback duties in 1966, he sparked his teammates to a perfect 11-0 record.

That year, his junior season, the Foley, Alabama, na-

Ken Stabler, All-American quarterback, 1967.

tive amassed 1,353 yards total offense, broke the S.E.C. passing percentage record and tossed nine touchdown passes. His 74 completions in 114 attempts gave him a percentage of 64.9.

Stabler climaxed a memorable 1966 season by winning the Most Valuable Player trophy for his performance in the 34-7 smashing of Nebraska in the Sugar Bowl. He hit on 12 of 17 passes for 218 yards, including a 45-yard touchdown to Ray Perkins. He also added 40 yards rushing.

In 1967, a defensive breakdown resulted in an 8-2-1 Tide record but Stabler's statistics remained impressive. He completed 103 of 178 passes, 57.9 per cent, for 1,214 yards and nine touchdowns.

When Bart Starr finally stepped down as quarterback at Green Bay, his replacement was Scott Hunter, who had just left Alabama's passing records in a shambles in 1970.

Scott Hunter hands off to Johnny Musso, All-American halfback, 1971.

The 6-foot-2, 203-pound athlete from Vigor High School in Prichard, Alabama, a suburb of Mobile, started dazzling opponents with his passing arm in 1968 as a sophomore and never stopped. In his first year he completed 122 of 227 for 1,471 yards and 10 touchdowns. His junior year was even better with 157 on target in 266 attempts for 2,188 yards and nine touchdowns.

Hunter finished his career with 382 completions for 4,899 yards and 34 touchdowns. His records included most passes attempted, most completed, most yards total offense for one season (junior year) and the S.E.C. mark for most yards gained passing in one game, 484 against Auburn in 1969. The same season, he also set the conference record for highest completion percentage when he hit 22 of 29 for 75.9 percent against Ole Miss.

Tide of All-Americans

From the time Coach Bryant arrived at Alabama in 1958 through the 1973 season, Alabama counted 27 players who were given recognition as All-Americans.

Following is a review of this honor roll:

Billy Neighbors (1961)

Neighbors, a 229-pound muscleman from Northport, Alabama, ranks as one of Bryant's best all-around linemen. He was one of the foremost blockers in the country and a devastating tackle on a defensive unit that ranked as the best in college football.

Lee Roy Jordan (1961 and 1962)

Jordan is the measure by which all Alabama defensive players are judged.

Although weighing only 207 pounds, he played center on offense and a linebacker on defense.

Billy Neighbors,
All-American tackle, 1961.

With Jordan leading the interior defense there was not a single opponent in 1961 or 1962 that managed more than seven points. He was voted Lineman of the Year in 1962 by the Birmingham Touchdown Club and also was selected Outstanding Lineman of the 1960 Bluebonnet Bowl, and the Outstanding Player in the 1963 Orange Bowl.

David Ray (1964)

Ray's valuable right toe provided the Crimson Tide with 109 points in 1964 and 1965. Several times his extra points and field goals spelled the difference between victory and defeat for the national champs.

In 1964, Ray set a National Collegiate Athletic Association record for scoring by kicking when he hit 23 of 25 extra points and 12 of 17 field goals for 59 points. (It has since been surpassed).

David Ray,
All-American halfback, 1964.

Ray also caught 19 passes for the 1964 squad, second on the team, for 271 yards. And his three pass interceptions led the defensive team.

Ray drilled seven of fourteen field goal tries in 1965 and 21 of 23 extra points. He also added one touchdown as a halfback. He was cited as an All-American both as a flanker and placekicker.

Dan Kearley (1964)

This husky tackle was an exceptionally strong and deceptively agile performer who played both offense and defense.

Anchoring the defensive front, Kearley was one big reason why opponents scored only 67 points in his All-American season.

As a right tackle on offense, he was credited for opening the path for many Crimson runners.

Dan Kearley,
All-American tackle, 1964.

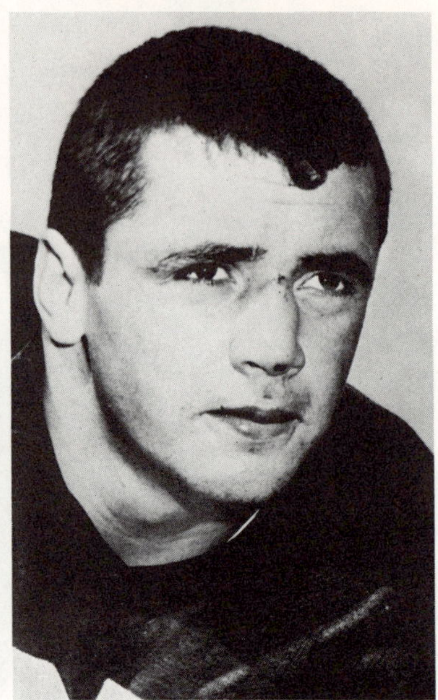

Wayne Freeman,
All-American guard, 1964.

Wayne Freeman (1964)

Namath was able to stand in the pocket and rifle the passes that made him famous because of the protection provided by right guard Freeman and his associates.

The 6-foot, 192-pound native of Fort Payne, Alabama, had fine speed for a lineman and was versatile enough to play offensive tackle when needed and was a tough defensive lineman.

Paul Crane (1965)

When Bryant presented Crane jersey number 54, one knew the crafty headmaster considered the Crimson Tide center-linebacker someone special. That was the number Lee Roy Jordan wore and Bryant has seldom praised any of his players more than Jordan.

"Crane is our finest all-around football player,"

Paul Crane, All-American center, 1965.

Bryant said. And that wasn't small praise because Crane played alongside five All-Americans in 1964 and 1965.

Crane, at 191 pounds, was another small lineman who compensated for his size with quickness and toughness, attributes which became synonymous with Alabama linemen.

Ray Perkins (1966)

Tuscaloosa football fans still rave about the kangaroo catches made by sure-handed receiver Ray Perkins during his record-setting career from 1964 through 1966.

The consensus All-American who later played with the Baltimore Colts, caught 77 passes and scored 12 touchdowns. In the 1966 Orange Bowl he had nine receptions and two touchdowns in the first half, setting a Bowl record and helping the Crimson to a 39-28 victory over Nebraska.

Ray Perkins, All-American offensive end, 1966.

Perkins clicked with Namath on a 20-yard touchdown pass in Alabama's 21-17 loss to Texas in the 1965 Orange Bowl. Bryant considered him with his 9.8 speed, the finest athlete on the team.

"I'm sure Ray could have been a star defensive back too," Bryant said.

Cecil Dowdy (1966)

Bryant rated Dowdy "among the top three finest blockers I've ever coached."

Dowdy graded high consistently throughout his career as the interior anchor on national championship clubs in 1964 and 1965. The bulk of the rushing success came over and through his tackle spot.

The 6-foot, 206-pounder was outstanding in the 1966 Orange Bowl.

Cecil Dowdy, All-American
offensive tackle, 1966.

Richard Cole, All-American
defensive tackle, 1966.

Richard Cole (1966)

The coaches expected Cole, a 6-foot, 196-pound defensive tackle, to do well in 1966, but he exceeded all expectations, using his quickness and ruggedness to gain All-American honors.

"Richard was a great leader," Assistant Coach Pat Dye said. "When the fourth quarter came along, you could count on Richard to make the key third down tackle or dump the passer for a loss on third down."

Bobby Johns (1966 and 1967)

This defensive halfback was considered one of the finest pass defenders and pass-theft artists in Tide history.

He was an integral part of the "greatest college team I've seen," according to Bryant, who was describing his 1966 club.

Bobby Johns, All-American
defensive halfback, 1966 and 1967.

Johns' finest hour came in the 1967 Sugar Bowl when the 180-pound native of Birmingham intercepted three Nebraska passes and returned them 19 yards. It tied the bowl record for interceptions set by Raymond Brown of Mississippi.

He stole four passes in 1966, returning two of them for touchdowns against Vanderbilt and Louisiana State. The previous fall Johns intercepted six passes, tying for the conference lead. That performance enabled him to become the first Tide sophomore to gain All-S.E.C. recognition since Harry Gilmer in 1945.

Dennis Homan (1967)

This lean whippet with sure hands still owned many Tide receiving records even after later onslaughts by outstanding pass catchers George Ranager, David Bailey and Wayne Wheeler.

Dennis Homan, All-American split end, 1967.

Homan's eighteen touchdowns from 1965 through 1967 stand as a career record as does his 820 yards receiving in 1967. He was especially dangerous as a long threat scoring seven touchdowns on pass plays of 50 yards or more.

He speared a 79-yarder from Ken Stabler in 1966 against Louisiana Tech and broke loose on a 65-yard pass play from Steve Sloan against Mississippi State in 1965. He wound up with 87 catches for 1,495 yards.

Sam Gellerstedt (1968)

Gellerstedt played only one fall at Alabama before transferring to the University of Tampa, but in that year gained the unusual distinction of earning All-American honors as a sophomore middle guard.

Nicknamed the "Little Samurai", the 5-foot-8, 195-pound lineman had the strength and speed to penetrate opposing backfields so quickly that he disrupted plays even when he didn't make the tackle.

Mike Hall (1968)

The "Football News" named Hall the outstanding linebacker in America in 1968 and Bryant rated him almost in the same class as Jordan.

His finest performance came against Auburn in 1968 when he made sixteen tackles, intercepted two passes (one of them leading to 'Bama's first touchdown), and then switched to offense and caught a five-yard touchdown pass from Scott Hunter to spark the 24-16 victory.

Against Clemson he made twelve tackles and assisted on twelve others. During the '68 season he intercepted five passes, recovered two fumbles, caused five other fumbles and blocked a punt against Ole Miss that was recovered for a touchdown.

Mike Hall,
All-American linebacker, 1968.

Alvin Samples,
All-American guard, 1969.

Alvin Samples (1969)

Samples was a bull-necked, 219-pound offensive guard who graded consistently high with his rugged blocking. "And he had excellent speed and quickness and was a football player from the word go," maintained Assistant Coach Jimmy Sharpe.

Samples played defensive tackle and guard throughout his sophomore season and part of his junior year before being switched to offense.

Johnny Musso (1970 and 1971)

Musso earned more trophies than any player in Alabama history and was called by Bryant "the greatest back I've ever coached."

Twice an All-American, the "Italian Stallion" was a

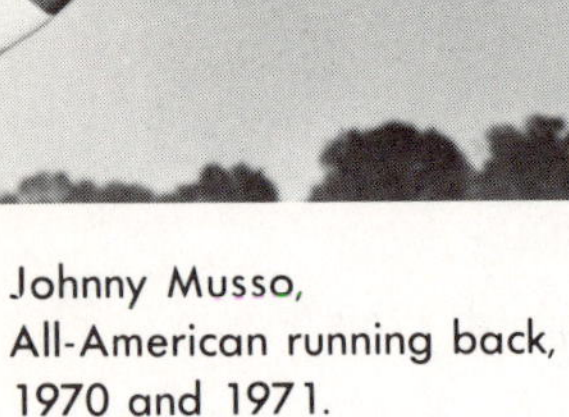

Johnny Musso,
All-American running back,
1970 and 1971.

Robin Parkhouse,
All-American defensive end, 1971.

gutty short yardage runner, a devastating blocker on out-side sweeps and fine passer on frequent halfback options.

He set eight S.E.C. records and 14 University marks, gaining 2,741 yards and scoring 38 touchdowns. He averaged an all-time S.E.C. record 91.4 yards per game.

Musso, the College Player of the Year in 1971 by vote of the "Football News," pointed to Alabama's 31-7 victory over arch-rival Auburn that gave 'Bama the conference crown as the game he remembered most. In that battle of the unbeatens, Musso gained 167 yards, scored twice, blocked savagely and did it all despite being on crutches ten days before the game.

Robin Parkhouse (1971)

Gained acclaim as the top defensive end in the S.E.C. and All-American honors as a senior.

Known as the "Pink Panther," Parkhouse was an out-

Tom Surlas,
All-American linebacker, 1971.

standing pass rusher, making nine behind-the-line stops for minus 50 yards as a senior. And he was rarely challenged by running plays to his side, making many of his stops in the middle of the line.

His senior season he knocked down six passes on the goal line, recovered two fumbles and forced four others.

Tom Surlas (1971)

Surlas, a weakside linebacker, played only one full season for Alabama but made it a memorable one.

"I came to Alabama because Coach Paul Bryant is willing to work with small but good football players," the 198-pound Surlas, a junior college transfer, said. "I'm sorry I let Coach Bryant and the team down as a junior when I got hurt and started feeling sorry for myself. I should have been trying all the harder. It made me more determined to do well as a senior."

Surlas led Tide tacklers with 45 stops, 46 assists, intercepted two passes, caused three fumbles, broke up several passes and was among the leaders in quarterback "sacks."

John Hannah (1971 and 1972)

"John Hannah's the best offensive lineman I've been around in 30 years of coaching," Bryant said of this 265-pound guard.

He won Lineman of the Year awards in 1971 and '72 for his size, quickness, and agility.

Hannah was a rare three-sport letterman, going unbeaten as a freshman wrestler, then switching to track where he won S.E.C. titles in the shot and discus.

John Mitchell (1972)

Bryant's recruiting forays into a previously untapped area—the junior colleges—began paying rich dividends in the 70s and Mitchell was a good example.

The 235-pound defensive end from Mobile earned Junior All-American honors at Eastern Arizona Junior College in 1970, then transferred to Tuscaloosa and became a major college All-American.

He teamed with Parkhouse to form a formidable defensive end combination. Mitchell stopped twelve backs behind the scrimmage line for losses of 81 yards and recovered a fumble that set up the winning touchdown in Alabama's come-from-behind victory at Tennessee.

Jim Krapf (1972)

A remarkable athlete, Krapf earned high honors at three different positions. He was an All-S.E.C. sophomore team middle linebacker; gained All-S.E.C. recognition as an offensive tackle in his junior year and finally was an

John Hannah,
All-American guard, 1971 and 1972.

John Mitchell,
All-American defensive end, 1972.

All-American center in 1972.

He led his team in tackles as a sophomore then was shifted to offensive tackle ten days before the 1971 season opener against Southern Cal. Alabama won 17-13 and Krapf's quickness at pulling out to block was one reason Alabama successfully switched to the wishbone formation in 1971.

Buddy Brown (1973)

Brown replaced Hannah as the leader of the interior line and in the words of Tide Center Sylvester Croom "he led by example."

Brown compiled the highest grades at offensive tackle made by any Alabama player in recent history with the exception of Hannah. The 243-pound native of Florida was originally a defensive player but was converted to

Jim Krapf, All-American center, 1972.

Buddy Brown, All-American offensive tackle, 1973.

offense as a sophomore, playing both guard and tackle. He was strictly a tackle in 1973.

Wayne Wheeler (1973)

Wheeler, a lightning-quick wide receiver, complemented the Tide's awesome wishbone attack in 1972 and 1973.

"Sure we have talented running backs but Wayne has been the difference," said Tide Quarterback Gary Rutledge. "He's just a tremendous threat that keeps the defense honest. Keeps 'em from stacking the line."

Wheeler, with speed and good hands, was the top receiver in '72 and '73, catching 30 passes for 573 yards and seven touchdowns as a junior and 19 for 530 yards and three T.D.'s in his senior year. He averaged 22.7 yards per reception in 1973.

Wayne Wheeler, All-American
offensive end, 1973.

Woodrow Lowe,
All-American linebacker, 1973.

Woodrow Lowe (1973)

Lowe gained All-American recognition as a sophomore in 1973 from the Football Writers and the Newspaper Enterprises poll.

The bruising linebacker led the Tide with 86 tackles, more than twice as many as anyone else, and assisted on 46 others. Lowe also dumped six runners for losses, caused two fumbles, recovered one and intercepted three passes. Added to that impressive list was a blocked field goal attempt.

"I'd put Woodrow in a class with Lee Roy Jordan right now," Bryant said after the youngster's sophomore season. "And by his senior year Woodrow will be in a class of his own."

Section Three:
The Games

10

The Thin Red Line

A touchdown counted four points, a field goal was worth five, and the term was "extra points" because a conversion after the touchdown was worth two. Tickets cost 25 cents and the program was filled with detailed explanations and rules of the new game which few of the spectators understood. The players wore pants that had sparse padding, jerseys that had an extra layer of material on the elbows and, if they were fortunate, the athletes were protected by a full head of hair that had not been trimmed since the previous spring.

Under such conditions the University of Alabama played its first meaningful football game in the dead of winter.

1893: AUBURN 32, ALABAMA 22

The date was February 22 and Alabama considered this game (its first against college competition) the final one of its initial season, which began in the fall of 1892. Auburn, which had taken up the sport in 1891, regarded this as the opener of its 1893 season.

Regardless, the first confrontation of the state rivals in this strange but intriguing new sport drew 5,000 fans to Birmingham's Lakeview Park to watch the bruising effects of the flying wedge, the turtle-back wedge and the revolving wedges. They were all mass running plays that kept the two teams on a collision course all day and sent bodies flying. Touchdowns usually were scored when a back managed to avoid the central mass confusion and was able to get outside the ends.

Auburn's captain Daniels and halfback Dorsey were the game's stars along with halfback Dan Smith of Alabama. Each scored two touchdowns and gained over 120 yards, according to sketchy accounts.

Alabama, despite its lack of experience, gave Auburn a good test. Near the end of the first half Smith circled end on a 20-yard touchdown and when G. H. Kyzer kicked the goal, Alabama trailed only 14-12.

Dorsey opened the second half, however, by picking up an Alabama fumble and racing 65 yards for a touchdown, and Daniels followed with the first of his three conversions. Auburn led 20-12.

Guard W.G. Little, the man who introduced football to Tuscaloosa and organized this first team, scored for Alabama on a 30-yard "guard-around," and Kyzer's kick trimmed Auburn's lead to 20-18.

It took Auburn only a few minutes, however, to put the game out of reach on the running of Buckalew, Dorsey, Riggs and Daniels.

The crowd apparently loved the action because the game was delayed on occasions to clear the field of spectators and players, particularly after a spectacular 65-yard run by Daniels.

1894: ALABAMA 18, TULANE 6

The date was November 3 and the place was New Orleans for Alabama's first victory over a college team after four defeats in two years including two at the hands of Auburn.

And it was Alabama's 155-pound coach, Eli Abbott, who was the outstanding player. Alabama lost a 4-0 halftime lead and trailed 6-4 in the second half when Abbott went to work. He scored three touchdowns in the "space of a few minutes" to go along with his first half touchdown and for once it was actually true that a coach led his team to victory.

1894: ALABAMA 18, AUBURN 0

This was 'Bama's first victory over Auburn and it was filled with the feuding and fierce competition that would subsequently mark, and occasionally mar, the series.

Auburn charged that Alabama was using players who had been recruited from outside the University and who were not enrolled as students. The Tigers also maintained that Abbott and J.E. Shelley, a running back, were being given a salary. Alabama denied the charges and none of their players—or the coach—was disqualified. Shelley proceeded to score the first touchdown and Abbott tallied the last two, one on a spectacular 75-yard run.

1901: ALABAMA 6, TENNESSEE 6

The first battle between these two universities bore an indication of the intensity that would develop in the rivalry when the game, played in Birmingham, had to be stopped early in the second half because the 2,000 fans, enraged by two offsides penalties assessed against Alabama, swarmed onto the field and remained until it was too dark to play.

1903: ALABAMA 18, AUBURN 6

Alabama had not beaten Auburn since 1894, having lost four games in a row by the scores of 48-0, 53-5, 17-0, and 23-0. Things were expected to be no different in this meeting, the Tigers being considered prohibitive favorites. But Alabama was developing its first truly outstanding back in Auxford Burks, who led the lighter 'Bama squad to a stunning upset.

Again the game was marked by an unfortunate incident when Guard W.C. Oates of Alabama allegedly was kicked in the head deliberately by an Auburn player and knocked unconscious.

The 1904 season was punctuated by several developments. Alabama provided the opposition for Florida State in that school's first football game. Experience won for Alabama 29-0. Two weeks later Alabama won its first forfeit, from Mississippi A.&M., 10-5. A.&M. forfeited the contest by walking off the field in the second half, claiming the referee had lost count of the downs, giving Alabama a fifth down.

THE 1906 SEASON

Often there were developments that would be considered unique today. After the opening game of the zany 1906 season, which featured the introduction of the forward pass, Coach J.W.H. Pollard was so displeased with the work of his charges in the 6-0 victory over Maryville that he put them through a long scrimmage against the reserves immediately following the contest. A week later the Howard team's arrival in Tuscaloosa was delayed so the game was shortened to two 15-minute halves since it was so late in the afternoon. Alabama sustained numerous injuries in the game and asked that it be allowed to cancel the contest the following week against Vanderbilt. But the Commodores refused and whipped 'Bama 78-0, scoring 57 points in the first half primarily with the pass, which

Alabama had not seen in such concentration previously. One report described the passes as "many rainbows thrown at random with hopes."

Accounts of the 16-4 victory over Mississippi A.&M. the next week in Starkville accused fans of throwing rocks and sticks at the Alabama players and charged that the referee called time out and, while Alabama players were huddled, allowed A.&M. to kick a field goal unmolested for its only points. Then after Burks scored a touchdown, the referee reportedly turned to the A.&M. players and said: "That's a touchdown, boys. I'll have to let them have it."

On October 17 came another Auburn tussle and more charges of "ringer" emerged. Auburn maintained that Alabama tackle T.C. Sims was not a student but the Tigers had not filed the complaint far enough in advance of the game and it was not upheld.

1907: ALABAMA 6, AUBURN 6

This was a significant game, not because Coach Pollard opened the second half with his tricky new "Varsity Two-Step" formation but because of the debates which would erupt afterward causing the series to be interrupted for 41 years.

Accusations of "ringers" persisted on both sides and the feud grew to the point that neither side could agree on anything. Auburn wanted to increase the number of players on its team, campaigned to give them more expense money and demanded that an eastern referee be brought in to officiate future games. Alabama opposed all the propositions then relented on the size of the squad and expense money, but balked at the compromise plan of letting a committee choose the referee.

The argument raged into October before Alabama finally gave in on the final point. By then the schedules of both teams were full. Hard feelings on both sides simmered for years with neither school initiating any serious move to resolve the differences and revive the competition.

The last contest was a battle in which both sides resorted to every device within the rules to win. Pollard's "Varsity Two-Step" was an example. The choreography itself was complex. One observer described it:

"The team is divided into two parts. The left side of the line joins hands behind the line and the right side does likewise. The center faces the backfield. The line skips back into position and the backs follow to either the right or left at the signal of the quarterback. There is an element of surprise in the play that results in confusion on the part of the defense...it's as fancy and as dainty as a minuet."

In less than five minutes after the "Varsity Two-Step" was unveiled, Alabama scored, kicked the goal, and the game was tied. Alabama moved again but was stopped at the goal line. Then Auburn marched 75 yards only to be stalled in the game's final minute by what was described as Alabama's "Thin Red Line," a term that later would evolve into the team's modern nickname, the Crimson Tide.

1908: ALABAMA 9, HASKELL INDIANS 8

By all accounts this was the most exciting game the Thin Red Line played in its early years, primarily because Haskell was considered an overwhelming favorite in view of its experience and weight advantage which was reported to average 25 pounds per man heavier than Alabama.

Haskell moved at will against the Crimson until the Indians neared the Alabama goal. Then a combination of Alabama tenacity and the unusually rough tactics of the visitors ("they jumped on players with their knees, slugged and piled on"), which drew repeated penalties, stopped drives.

With five minutes left Haskell, which had totally dominated the contest, led 8-4. Then Guard G.W. Arant rushed the Indians' passer, deflected the pass into the arms of teammate B.B. Edwards, who picked up the ball at his shoetops and raced 65 yards for a touchdown (now worth five points) and Alabama's winning points.

1912: ALABAMA 10, MISSISSIPPI 9

This was the season the three Van de Graaff brothers played together for the Thin Red Line: senior Adrian, junior Hargrove and freshman Bully, who in 1915 would become Alabama's first All-American.

Alabama jumped to a 10-0 lead against a strong Mississippi team, then held on for dear life, to survive. Mississippi, led by Fletcher ("who seldom failed to gain Substantial amounts ... and between halves casually smoked cigarettes") relentlessly marched at the Crimson but scored only nine points.

1915: ALABAMA 23, SEWANEE 10

There were other significant games for Alabama in the interim including the 6-0 triumph over Tennessee in 1913 that was concluded in darkness with the headlights from automobiles illuminating the field. And there was the upset of Georgia Tech 13-0 in 1914. But the most important victory prior to 1920 was the Crimson's first decision over Sewanee, the power of the South.

Alabama had not beaten Sewanee in 21 years and in this particular meeting was without Coach Thomas Kelly, who had contracted typhoid fever. Athletic Director Lonnie Noojin took command of the team.

Fortunately All-American Bully Van de Graaff was healthy and almost single-handedly carried the Crimson to a tense victory that saw 23 points scored in the final quarter, 13 by Bully. Four times in the third quarter alone 'Bama successfully made goal-line stands but on the first play of the fourth quarter Sewanee scored and moments later blocked a punt setting up the tying field goal.

The Mountain Tigers were moving relentlessly for another score late in the game when Van de Graaff rushed the Sewanee passer, blocked the pass, caught it before it hit the ground and raced 65 yards for the winning touchdown. Van de Graaff kicked two more field goals in the final moments.

1919: ALABAMA 50, MISSISSIPPI 0

It was games such as this romp that inspired the *Birmingham News'* Zipp Newman to describe Alabama as the Crimson Tide. Led by Riggs Stephenson, 'Bama shut out seven of nine opponents this season, rolled up 280 points while yielding only 22 for an 8-1 record and reminded Newman of the ocean tide which kept relentlessly pounding away. It was obvious the team no longer could be referred to as the Thin Red Line. Thus Coach Xen Scott's crimson-jersied athletes earned the lasting title of the Crimson Tide.

11

Alabama Discovered-
in Philadelphia

Since 1903, when Alabama last suffered a losing season, the Crimson Tide had compiled an enviable record of 83 victories, 35 losses, and nine ties entering the 1920s. But news of their prowess was slow to penetrate even the southern region and nationally they attracted little notice.

The team had played just one intersectional game of note and it was in Alabama in 1908 against Cincinnati. Alabama won 16-0 and displayed individual talent in players such as Henry Burks (brother of Auxford), Derrill Pratt, Center C.C. Countess and passer E.B. Peebles, but little was made of the victory and a certain obscurity tended to surround succeeding Alabama triumphs.

That condition was changed, however, in the 1920s under the guidance of Coaches Xen Scott and Wallace Wade.

1920: ALABAMA 14, VANDERBILT 7

Alabama's schedule was expanded to eleven games

with the addition of its first contest outside the South in Cleveland, Ohio, against Case.

This would also be Alabama's first ten-victory season and included its first triumph ever over Vanderbilt, which had won all five previous meetings. All the scoring was accomplished in the first half and most of the Crimson offense was handled by Riggs Stephenson and E.B. Lenoir.

Late in the first quarter Alabama began a 70-yard scoring march with Stephenson accounting for nearly 45 yards including the final four. A few minutes later Alabama put together another long march. Stephenson burst free for gains of nine and 20 yards. Then Lenoir scored in four rushes covering 33 yards.

Late in the first half Vanderbilt recovered a bad center snap at the 'Bama 10. Three plays later Jess Neely, who would later gain fame as head coach at Rice and Clemson and serve as Vanderbilt's athletic director, grabbed a touchdown pass and the Crimson's hard-earned lead was suddenly cut in half.

From there on the Crimson defense held to preserve the 14-7 victory that was a significant step in its rise to football fame.

1920: GEORGIA 21, ALABAMA 14

Georgia scored none of its points on offense this day. The remarkable tallies developed in the first five minutes and the final five minutes. Two plays after the opening kickoff, Lenoir fumbled and the ball popped into the arms of Georgia's Page Bennett who rambled 40 yards for the touchdown. Alabama was unable to move when it got the ball back and Stephenson's punt was blocked by Welchel. Again the fickle ball found the waiting arms of a Georgia player, who ran 25 yards for the score providing the Bulldogs with a 14-0 lead.

In the third quarter Alabama finally found some luck of its own. Stephenson, from his own 24-yard line, attempted a pass. A Georgia player tipped the ball but it deflected into the arms of end Al Clemens who raced 76 yards with the aid of good blocking to score, pulling Alabama even.

With time running out, the Tide attempted a 20-yard field goal but Georgia blocked it, grabbed the ball in mid air, and sprinted 80 yards for the game-winning touchdown.

It was a bitter defeat but the Tide didn't have time to dwell on the upset. Six days later the Crimson were en route for the first time to a date north of the Mason-Dixon line.

1920: ALABAMA 40, CASE 0

Coach Scott had graduated from Western Reserve in Cleveland and had worked for a Cleveland newspaper as a sportswriter during the summer months. With numerous contacts in the city he set up a game in Cleveland against Case.

If the Crimson Tide was weary from its busy schedule and the trek north, it never gave a hint. Stephenson passed for more than 100 yards, scored two touchdowns and Lenoir and Clemens also scored twice. Instead of Alabama tiring it was Case that bogged down in the final quarter when the Tide scored three times to complete the rout.

Perhaps the impressive victory didn't stand all of Yankeeland on its ear but Stephenson left some impressions in Cleveland about his general athletic ability and by the spring of 1921, even before graduation ceremonies, the star running back was in the baseball uniform of the Cleveland Indians.

1921: ALABAMA 14, TULANE 7

The prestige that Alabama gained in 1920 was almost

lost in 1921 when its first losing season in 18 years was averted only by upsetting Tulane 14-7 in the final game of the season in New Orleans.

The game ended in a riot when Tulane scored on what appeared to be the last play of the game. But the referee ruled that the final whistle had sounded before the ball had been snapped. The Alabama players were walking off the field and had taken off their helmets as Tulane was scoring. The fans poured onto the field pursuing the referee, and it required two dozen policemen to subdue them and provide the official with an escort safely out of the stadium.

1922: ALABAMA 9, PENNSYLVANIA 7

For the first time in the school's history it was sending a team into the northeast, hotbed of football, to tackle an outstanding University of Pennsylvania team. Scott was taking a travel-weary squad on the 2,500-mile trip from Austin, Texas, to Philadelphia and he was growing increasingly weaker each day with his serious illness.

It was a demanding journey by train and the players thought it was merely a considerate gesture on the part of Scott to break the trip in Washington and allow them to visit Griffith Stadium where Navy, which had just lost to Penn, defeated Penn State 14-0.

But Scott and Athletic Director Charlie Bernier had a more important reason for stopping. As Zipp Newman, who made the trip to cover the team for the *Birmingham News,* later recalled:

"We all came away from the game with the idea that neither team was that great. We just didn't think much of the football they played. It was a smart move on Scott's part."

He had overcome a difficult mental hurdle for his team even before it stepped onto Franklin Field before 25,000 Penn fans and 500 Alabama loyalists who made the trip. It was the largest audience that had ever seen the Crimson Tide.

Late in the first period Charles Bartlett fired a long pass to little W.C. Baty, the smallest player on the field who later would become Alabama's team physician and county health officer in Tuscaloosa. It set up Bull Wesley's field goal and, surprisingly, Penn trailed 3-0.

The lead didn't last long. A short Alabama punt put Penn just 35 yards from the end zone and one play later George Sullivan burst through to the 15, reversed his field, and raced in for a touchdown and Penn led 7-3.

But Penn had trouble making further headway and its frustration began to tell in the third quarter when Thurman, its All-American tackle, started slugging Baty on every play. Finally the referee spotted the illicit rough stuff, penalized Penn, and ejected Thurman.

Baty and his teammate later reflected that the game turned on that incident.

Finally a Penn punt reached only to its own 27-yard line and Bartlett sprinted outside end for 23 yards. Three plays from the four-yard line failed to gain but on the last down, two of Alabama's finest performers, Pooley Hubert and Center Clyde (Shorty) Propst, combined for the Crimson Tide's most important, if not artistic, touchdown. Hubert barged into the end zone but fumbled. Propst outscrambled Penn defenders to recover and 'Bama led 9-7.

Alabama had its first victory that would draw national attention. Most followers have agreed this one game not only put Alabama on the football map but earned a new measure of respect for the quality of the sport in the South.

When the victorious Tide returned to Tuscaloosa there was a huge celebration and the following week thousands jammed into the campus field to watch Alabama destroy L.S.U. 47-3. Now the state's zest for football was growing rapidly.

The next season, 1923, introduced the Wallace Wade era that in just three years would have Alabama making a lasting name for itself in the Rose Bowl.

Wade's teams needed many important games, however, to hone their skills before the Rose Bowl glories could be realized, and the new coach later recalled that none was more significant than the third contest of his first season. It was played in Syracuse, New York, and Alabama took its first and worst beating in Wade's eight-year tenure at the Capstone.

1923: SYRACUSE 23, ALABAMA 0

Alabama had lost seven starters from the previous season and was still learning the Wade single-wing system. The Tide, however, managed to slip by Union 12-0 in the opener and manhandled Mississippi 56-0.

Spirits were high as they embarked on the 1,800-mile journey north, remembering their success the previous fall in Philadelphia. But this time they would be encountering a much stronger team. Syracuse had lost only ten games in six years and would not be caught unaware as Penn had been.

Although unable to generate an offense against the experienced Orangemen, the Tide made a close game of it throughout the first half. At intermission Syracuse led only 3-0 and the two defenses might have kept it a tight battle except for three Alabama mistakes. First, Red Barnes fumbled near midfield and a Syracuse defender took the ball for a touchdown. The Tide failed to cover a punt early in the fourth period, and it was returned 70 yards for a score. Finally, an interception set up a touchdown.

Wade said the loss taught him more about football than any other game he coached.

1924: ALABAMA 55, UNION 0

A sophomore running back named Johnny Mack Brown scored three touchdowns in this opening game and Alabama fans realized they had discovered something special.

The Tide won a week later from Furman 20-0, and Brown intercepted a pass and ran it 58 yards for a T.D. Three weeks later he showed his brilliance in leading the Tide to an impressive 14-0 victory over Georgia Tech in Atlanta. Brown gained 135 yards in 10 carries and caught a 37-yard touchdown pass from Gillis.

Brown dazzled the homecoming crowd in Tuscaloosa the following Saturday with a 99-yard kickoff return in the 47-7 romp over Kentucky.

Now Alabama had a star and Wade had developed an impressive collection of athletes to complement Brown. The Crimson rolled to an 8-1 record in 1924, the year being marred only by a 17-0 upset to Centre College, which completely shut off Brown and did not permit the Tide to penetrate further than Centre's 48-yard line.

But Wade would suffer no such surprises in 1925, the year which stands above all others in the development of Alabama football. It led to the Rose Bowl.

This was an outstanding group of players: names such as Brown, Hubert, Barnes, Caldwell, Gillis, Little Dave Rosenfeld, Winslett, Jones, Buckler, Holmes, and Pickhard.

They were awesome while marching undefeated through nine regular season opponents. Only one team scored against them and that was Birmingham Southern, which was a 50-7 victim.

1925: ALABAMA 7, GEORGIA TECH 0

The unbeaten giants of the south clashed in the game that would establish Wade as one of the nation's outstand-

Freddie Pickhard, Alabama tackle and team captain, 1927.

ing coaches. It was also a stage for the tremendous running abilities of Brown and the brilliant blocking, running, and defensive work of Hubert, who most observers felt played his finest game this day. Brown, in fact, was so slippery on the soggy Grant Field turf in Atlanta that allegations were made that he wore rubber pants during the game.

The lone touchdown was a work of art. Brown dropped back to receive a punt early in the third quarter. Hubert retreated as the ball was punted to provide protection and just as Tech's ends were converging on Brown, Hubert made a diving block that wiped out both men and sprung Brown who turned to his left and began sprinting down the sidelines. His teammates eliminated would-be tacklers, and as Brown stepped into the end zone completing his 55-yard gallop he looked back and surveyed an incredible scene of destruction. All 11 Tech defenders—plus the referee—were in various prone positions having been knocked off their feet either by the interference or by Brown's magnificent moves.

Alabama felt it had overcome the last big hurdle toward an unbeaten season, but the Tide quickly discovered the next week that such thinking can be dangerous.

1925: ALABAMA 6, MISSISSIPPI A.&M. 0

The Tide received a real scare in a driving rain and needed a short A.&M. punt to set up that lone score. It traveled only to the A.&M. 26-yard line. Hubert and Jimmy Johnson alternated smashing the line until Hubert tossed an eight-yard touchdown pass to Winslett. Still the Tide needed a pass interception late in the game at the goal line by Caldwell to prevent a tie or loss.

The rest was relatively simple. Kentucky fell 31-0 with Brown scoring on a 79-yard run and his brother, Red, racing 75 yards with a fumble recovery for another touchdown. Alabama used its passing game to rip Florida 34-0 with Johnny Mack catching two touchdown tosses and Lovely Barnes scoring twice.

Then came the critical day—November 26—when all of Alabama realized that an impressive victory might earn the Tide a Rose Bowl invitation. Georgia was the opponent and Alabama forgot its conservative approach, trotted out triple and double passes, reverses, and thoroughly tangled the Bulldogs in trickery for a 27-0 triumph and ultimately the coveted ticket to Pasadena.

12

Wars for Roses

The argument still rages as to whether the 1926 Rose Bowl was the most exciting in the history of the spectacle, but there seems to be no doubt it was Alabama's finest hour. Wallace Wade had been working toward this date for three seasons. University President Mike Denny had pressed for such recognition for 13 years, and it was the culmination of all the school's efforts in the sport since its first day of competition in 1892.

Alabama left its mark in dramatic fashion. Washington, led by its remarkable All-American back George Wilson, built up a 12-0 halftime lead. But Wilson missed 22 minutes of the second half because of injuries, and during that time, Pooley Hubert, Johnny Mack Brown, and Grant Gillis combined to trigger a 20-point Crimson Tide explosion that resulted in the eventual 20-19 victory.

Damon Runyon wrote that this Alabama team

University of Alabama varsity, 1925.

"probably [was] the greatest that ever came out of the South."

But the Crimson Tide had arrived in Southern California on Christmas Eve after a six-day train trip without any such reputation. Californians were hospitable almost to a fault, inviting them to tour the city, the Pacific beaches, movie studios, and arranging parties. But they didn't think much of Alabama football. Washington ranked a ten-point favorite the day the Tide stepped off the train.

Wade hadn't embarked on this nearly 3,000-mile journey to come back empty-handed and it didn't take long for his West Coast hosts to realize how serious the Alabama coach was about winning. They had the mistaken notion that these southerners should have been satisfied with just making an appearance in the Pasadena classic. But Wade scheduled a practice on Christmas Day, and after four days of sight-seeing, which was fitted around the daily workouts, the coach ordered "no more entertainment."

As New Year's Day approached observers at the Alabama practice sessions grew more and more impressed with the precision, strength, and organization of the Tide and the talents of such individuals as Hubert, Brown, and Gillis. The odds began gradually dropping and by game time Washington was only a slight favorite.

Speculation continues even today that if the game's greatest individual performer, Wilson, had remained healthy Washington would have defeated what was obviously a better all-around team in Alabama.

Wilson, who had been offered $3,000 a month earlier to turn pro, clearly was the dominant factor while he was on the field. He had come to the University in a package deal along with his high school coach Enoch Bagshaw from Everett, Washington. Bagshaw was named head coach and Wilson soon was named the team.

Against Alabama he played little more than half the game, yet gained 134 yards in 15 carries, was never stopped behind the line, and only twice failed to gain yardage. He ripped off gains of 36, 21, 17, and 11 yards twice.

Defensively, Wilson also controlled things. Early in the game the Crimson Tide marched to the Washington 15-yard line. There, on second down, Wilson met Johnny Mack Brown head-on and tossed him for a two-yard loss. On the next play fullback Emile Barnes was blasted by Wilson and a blitzing line resulting in an eight-yard loss.

On fourth down, Wilson intercepted a Winslett pass at the Washington six yard line and raced 40 yards putting in motion the Huskies' first touchdown drive.

Near the end of the first quarter Wilson was knocked unconscious while tackling Winslett but was revived, stayed in the game, and shortly afterward boomed a 63-

yard punt into the end zone; Gillis punted back to the Washington 41, and Wilson set the second scoring drive going with a 36-yard scamper. Only an open-field tackle by Brown saved a T.D. On the next play Wilson passed to Cole for the touchdown and Washington had a 12-0 lead.

Midway in the second quarter, however, Wilson was knocked unconscious for the second time and on this occasion he had to be removed from the game.

Wade had changed tactics at halftime, switching emphasis in his running game from Brown to Hubert.

During the 22 minutes Wilson had been out of the game, Washington had gained only 17 yards and had been outscored 20-0. Finally, in desperation, Bagshaw sent Wilson back into the game when Alabama was threatening to score again at the Washington 18-yard line early in the fourth quarter. Wilson helped stop the drive at the 12, the Huskies took over and on the first play the irrepressible Wilson rambled 17 yards. The inspired Huskies moved quickly for a score, which came on a 27-yard pass from Wilson to Guttormsen. It was his second touchdown pass and his fifth completion of the day for a total of 77 yards.

But when the Alabama defense had to stop the gallant Wilson late in the fourth quarter, it rose to the test. Twice the Tide intercepted Wilson passes, including one brilliant grab by Gillis, and the Huskies were never able to penetrate Alabama territory again.

The first chapter of college football's most prolific bowl team thus was written. From that time until New Year's Eve 1973, when the Tide met Notre Dame in the Sugar Bowl, Alabama football teams accepted invitations to 27 bowl games, a record no other school could match.

1926: ALABAMA 21, GEORGIA TECH 0

This was a triumph for the Tide's rugged line, which

held Tech to two first downs, and for Winslett, the end who the Yellow Jackets figured could pass only to Caldwell.

Set up on the Tech 35-yard line by an exchange of punts in the first quarter, Winslett unveiled his running game. He ran a reverse handoff to Caldwell for a first down and hit the line himself for three yards. He passed to Caldwell for eleven more, then faked a deep pass to Caldwell, who drew the defenders to one side of the field and instead tossed to Melvin (Snake) Vines for the touchdown. Later Winslett also passed to Tolbert H. Brown setting up a score and found Archie Taylor for the other touchdown pass.

The stunning victory, however, almost caused the Crimson Tide to be upset the following week.

1926: ALABAMA 2, SEWANEE 0

Five times the Crimson Tide marched deep into Sewanee territory and in the final moments had a first down at the Mountain Tigers' one-yard line. Four line plunges failed to get the touchdown and it appeared Alabama's fifteen-game winning streak was about to end. But in the final 60 seconds, the Tide's great line put on a massive rush, successfully blocked a Sewanee punt and the ball rolled through the end zone for a safety.

That was the last really close call for the Crimson Tide. The defense allowed only six points in the last six games, held Kentucky to only 35 yards rushing in a 14-0 victory, and when Alabama defeated Georgia 33-6 on Thanksgiving Day, it had wrapped up its third consecutive Southern Conference championship and its second Helms Foundation award—symbolic of the national champs.

Later that evening the Rose Bowl called again wondering if the Wonders of the South would be interested in trying to repeat their miraculous effort of last New Year's Day.

1927: ALABAMA 7, STANFORD 7

That the Crimson Tide was able to emerge with a draw was a miracle of sorts because it required a blocked punt in the final four minutes, an Alabama touchdown four plays before the end of the game and an audacious bit of chicanery on the extra point.

But the game itself was hardly one to match the battle with Washington a year earlier. One writer referred to it as "frowsy football," and there was some question as to whether it was Alabama's defense or Stanford's offensive ineptness near the Crimson Tide goal line that kept the California team from romping to victory.

Four times Stanford moved inside the Alabama 10 yard line but came away with only one touchdown—an 18-yard pass near the end of the first quarter from George Bogue, who rarely threw, to Ed Walker, who had not caught a pass all year.

Alabama, by contrast, had its one opportunity late in the fourth quarter set up when Alabama center Clarke Pearce blocked a punt by substitute Frankie Wilton. It rolled more than 25 yards to the Stanford 14-yard line.

Wallace Wade, ever the psychologist, then surprised the crowd of 58,000 by sending 170-pound Jimmy Johnson into the game. Johnson had been hampered by a dislocated shoulder and had played little the last two seasons. But Wade's players had great respect for Johnson's fortitude as well as his talents. Johnson gave them the spark they needed. Winslett battered for three yards to the eleven; then Johnson sliced thru for seven to the four. Winslett tried the line twice and moved the ball to the one from where Johnson scored.

Stanford had outgained Alabama in total net yards 305 to 98, had twelve first downs to six for the Crimson Tide, yet now, in the lengthening shadows, the southern

Tony Holm,
All-American fullback, 1929.

invaders had a chance to pull even.

Wade, of course, had another little touch to ensure that the extra point was made. It was a play his club had rehearsed for just such an occasion.

The Crimson Tide broke from the huddle and lined up for the conversion attempt. Captain Lovely Barnes hesitated for a moment, then straightened up and barked: "Signals-off." The Stanford players, hearing the instructions, relaxed and looked at Barnes. At that instant Gordon Holmes centered the ball to Winslett who casually placed the ball down and Rosy Caldwell, unmolested, lined up the ball and kicked it through the uprights. The scoreboard said 7-7 and three plays later the 13th Rose Bowl game was over.

There were times, of course, when defeats simply could not by avoided and the following season four of them plagued Wade's team, which had suffered from graduation losses—particularly in the backfield.

1927: GEORGIA TECH 13, ALABAMA 0

This was the first loss for the Tide since 1924 and even then the victor was forced to struggle. Georgia Tech, which had been shut out by Alabama for the previous four years, finally scored in the second quarter when Stumpy Thomason skirted outside, cut back, and barged 30 yards for a touchdown.

Alabama outgained Tech 188 yards to 144 but had only one real scoring threat when Archie Taylor, despite being slowed by an injury, broke into the open on a 40-yard scamper. But he was caught from behind by Georgia Tech's Watkins at the 11-yard line and the Tide could move no further.

Georgia Tech got its final touchdown with only two minutes remaining after recovering an Alabama fumble on the Tide one-yard line.

Wade's forces rebounded for victories the next three Saturdays and faint hopes were aroused that maybe another Rose Bowl bid could be earned. But then came Wade's most disastrous streak in his eight years at the Capstone. The Tide lost the last three games of the season to Florida 13-6, Georgia 20-6, and Vanderbilt 14-7. In each case the Tide was the victim of great individual stars—"Cannon Ball" Clyde Crabtree of Florida, Roy Estes of Georgia, and Vanderbilt's All-American Bill Spears.

The losing streak signaled a period of doldrums, by Alabama standards, in 1928 and 1929 when the team had identical records of six victories and three losses. But the two years were not without their significant games, particularly the revival of the Tennessee rivalry after a 14-year lapse in 1928.

1928: TENNESSEE 15, ALABAMA 13

This was not, by any measure, a great day for Crimson Tide football but it was a significant day in the history of the sport regardless, because many observers felt that this victory for Tennessee at Tuscaloosa on homecoming day was the making of one of the most successful college coaches, General Robert Neyland.

Neyland's Volunteers were prohibitive underdogs this day but they shocked the Crimson Tide on the opening kickoff when Tennessee's great Gene McEver, inducted into the Hall of Fame in 1954, raced 98 yards for a touchdown and another Hall of Famer Bobby Dodd kicked the extra point.

In only four plays, however, Alabama had six of those points back on a 45-yard touchdown pass to John Suther. But Dodd twice punted the Tide deep into its own territory and finally a safety resulted when Suther fumbled a snap from center in the end zone while attempting to punt out of danger.

Tennessee led 9-6 after the first quarter and early in the second period McEver and Dodd went to work again. The Vols had a 15-6 lead and, aided by Alabama fumbles, held on for the victory. Neyland went on to post his second consecutive unbeaten season and his teams went undefeated in five of six years between 1927 and 1932.

1930: ALABAMA 18, TENNESSEE 6

In 1930, Wallace Wade finally had his athletes regrouped, although it was already known the coach would be leaving for Duke at season's end. He had some genuine stars again, including All-American Tackle Fred Sington, left-handed sophomore back Johnny Cain, John (Monk) Campbell, Flash Suther, and Jimmy Moore.

They stormed past their first three opponents, beating Howard 43-0, Mississippi 64-0 and Sewanee 25-0 before it was time to face Tennessee again on homecoming day for Alabama alumni. Denny Stadium was jammed with 18,000 fans who sensed this was the day that would reveal whether they had another champion emerging. Neyland's single-wing powerhouse had not lost a game since 1926 but three of its stars, McEver, Hug, and Brandt, were sidelined with injuries.

Wade pulled a ploy that he would use successfully again in the Rose Bowl against Washington State. He started his second stringers and they battled Tennessee on even terms until late in the first quarter when the Vols began a sustained march.

When the drive reached the Alabama 28-yard line, Wade called for his regulars, Sington, Campbell and Charlie Clement, and the Tennessee drive ground to a halt at the 10.

From there the Tide consumed 11 plays in a ground-oriented push that ended when Cain burst off tackle for 14 yards and a touchdown.

A few minutes later Suther sprinted 31 yards for another score and Alabama led 12-0. In the third quarter the Tide converted a fumble into an 18-0 lead then held off a furious Dodd passing blitz to win its most important game in four years.

1930: ALABAMA 13, GEORGIA 0

There were 28,000 fans in Birmingham for this game. It was Wade's last appearance as head coach of Alabama on home territory and there was a Rose Bowl trip at stake. Wade's greatest stroke of the day was simply being sure that Johnny Cain was in the starting lineup.

Cain was sensational. He gained 118 yards and set up one touchdown with a 24-yard scamper and scored the other late in the game. Cain also bombed the Bulldogs repeatedly back into their own ground with towering punts and was a demon linebacker on defense.

1931 Rose Bowl pre-game toss-up. Left, Alabama captain
Charles B. Clement. Right, Washington State captain Schwartz.

It all resulted in a memorable afternoon in Birmingham, the crowd's emotions building in a dramatic salute to Wade as the game ended. And then, later, they learned that Pasadena was calling again.

1931: ALABAMA 24, WASHINGTON STATE 0

As in 1926, there were laments about the opposition's loss of its star player being the reason for the Crimson Tide's resounding Rose Bowl victory.

Quarterback Bill Tonkin, who was also the Cougars' safety on defense, was flattened immediately after receiving a punt in the first quarter, a period which Washington State had controlled against Wade's reserves, who had been given a surprise starting assignment.

But the Tide proved this day that it was superior in most all aspects of the game and particularly in its vast quantity of quality talent.

The reserves had run every play on the ground through the first quarter. Then Wade inserted his No. 1 unit late in the first period and it found the Cougars primed for the kill.

At the Alabama 39-yard line, left end Jimmy Moore pulled out, circled back, and took a handoff from fullback Cain. Meanwhile, left half Flash Suther had streaked straight downfield. Moore halted short of the scrimmage line and hurled a long pass to the wide open Suther, who gathered in the ball at the Cougars' 22-yard line and sped untouched into the end zone.

Minutes later the alert Tide was in the Cougars' end zone again. Center Jess Eberdt picked off a short pass by Washington State's star halfback Tuffy Ellingsen at the Cougar 47. Monk Campbell barged for six yards, then the Crimson Tide called for the same play that had produced a touchdown a few moments earlier. Again Moore took the handoff from Cain and this time arched the ball for end Ben Smith, who was covered tightly by three defenders. But Smith leaped and came down with the ball on the one. Campbell scored on the next play.

The Crimson Tide needed only three more plays to shock the 60,000 in the Rose Bowl with a third touchdown. Campbell faked a handoff to Moore, bolted through left guard and wiggled 43 yards for the touchdown. Washington State coach Orin (Babe) Hollingbery called the second quarter "a nightmare" that haunted him for years afterward.

13

The 1930s Belong to Alabama

The decade of the 30s was one of the most vital and successful in the rapid rise of the Crimson Tide, rivaled only by the fabulous conquests of the 1960s.

Twice (in 1930 and 1934) Alabama was crowned national champions. The Southeastern Conference was formed from the unwieldy Southern Intercollegiate Conference in 1933 and Alabama won the first two S.E.C. championships.

Coach Frank Thomas molded a team in 1934 which many agreed was the mightiest football unit ever to represent the South. And it captured the Rose Bowl trophy with an impressive 29-13 victory over the Stanford Indians, which Zipp Newman referred to as "the greatest team I ever saw beaten." The brilliant passer and runner Dixie Howell and All-American end Don Hutson provided the Crimson Tide with one of the most dangerous aerial combinations in collegiate history. There were other stars such as Bill Lee, Riley Smith, Charlie Marr, Joe Demyanovich,

Riley Smith, All-American
quarterback, 1935.

and Bear Bryant.

Thomas had another Southeastern Conference champion in 1937. The Crimson Tide upset Southern California in 1938 and a year later surprised Fordham's famed Seven Blocks of Granite in New York's Polo Grounds 7-6.

It was the decade when Bryant played in a game despite a broken leg, when the new Denny Stadium was dedicated on the Tuscaloosa campus, when Alabama was shocked by a 7-7 tie with undermanned Howard College, and when it lost its only Rose Bowl.

The 1930s produced 89 victories, only 11 losses, and 4 ties. Four of the defeats and one of the ties we administered by arch-rival Tennessee and one of the most storied games of the period matched the Vols and the Tide in 1932.

1932: TENNESSEE 7, ALABAMA 3

Punting was the favorite weapon of the Volunteers under General Neyland. Neyland would even order punts on first down if he didn't like the field position. It was Neyland's contention that the opposition should be kept bottled up in its own end of the field until it inevitably made a mistake.

On this day, however, Frank Thomas had a left-footed punter who had Neyland looking down the barrel of his own gun. He was Johnny Cain and he more than matched Tennessee's great Beattie Feathers in a punting duel that is remembered more than any other in the South.

The conditions were such that punting was the soundest course of action. A heavy rain persisted throughout and it stymied almost everyone except Cain and Feathers. Cain punted 19 times and averaged 48 yards a kick. Feathers booted 21 times for a 43-yard average including an 18-yarder.

In the second quarter the Tide rolled 46 yards to the Tennessee six before the march stalled and Hillman Holley kicked a field goal.

The rain seemed to increase in intensity and neither team was able to mount an attack in the fourth quarter. Feathers dropped back for still another punt and it was magnificent. It soared to the Alabama five-yard line and rolled dead on the one.

Alabama knew it must kick out of danger immediately. But the ball was slippery, the pass from center was low and hit Cain in the knee. He barely got away a 12-yard punt. On third down, Feathers smashed off left tackle for the touchdown and a classic contest was decided.

1933: ALABAMA 12, TENNESSEE 6

If the loss in the rain was bitter, the victory the following fall in Knoxville for the Crimson Tide was deliciously sweet. The Volunteers hadn't lost at home since 1924 but few visitors ever brought to the Tennessee campus an athlete like Millard (Dixie) Howell. Already in his first three games at Alabama he had become a dominant force and he was destined to be the man around whom Coach Thomas would build the ultimate southern powerhouse the following season.

It wasn't easy, however. Tennessee, on a 12-yard touchdown run by Feathers in the second period, led 6-0 midway in the third quarter.

That's when Howell erupted. He had exploded his last two punts of the first half 65 and 85 yards and now he was about to display his other talents. First, he returned a punt 20 yard to the Vols' 44-yard line. He threw a pass to Larry Hughes for first down then pulled a beautiful fake, slipped the ball to Erskine Walker and drew the Vols to one side while Walker slipped into the end zone for the tying touchdown.

In the fourth quarter, Howell set up the winning score when he ran back a Feathers' punt to the Vols' 41. Walker raced for a first down and, after a penalty, moved the ball to the four. Howell scored.

That was hardly the end, though. Tennessee marched quickly to the Tide 38 with time running out. Feathers nearly got away for a touchdown but was stopped by Joe Demyanovich. A penalty moved Tennessee to the six and a first down. There guard Tom Hupke took over for the Tide. He stopped Feathers after a two-yard gain, then caught Brackett behind the line for a two-yard loss. Feathers, on third down, was thrown for a one-yard loss. A desperation fourth-down pass fell incomplete. Howell punted out of danger and time expired.

One week later the Crimson Tide gave another good accounting but suffered the only loss it would absorb over the next two seasons, a 2-0 setback to highly-rated

Dixie Howell,
All-American back, 1934.

Fordham before 60,000 in the Polo Grounds.

A fumbled punt set up the Rams deep in Alabama territory in the first period. The Rams' drive stalled at the two-yard line but Howell's punt was blocked and rolled out of the end zone for a safety. Twice late in the game Howell narrowly missed connecting with Don Hutson on touchdown passes.

Alabama went on to win the first Southeastern Conference championship and week by week Thomas came to realize the potential of his Howell-to-Hutson passing combination. His obvious plan was to build his 1934 edition around the pair. But even Thomas didn't realize how great they would become.

1934: ALABAMA 13, TENNESSEE 6

It was a talented team in all positions, and it easily crunched through Howard, Sewanee, and Mississippi

University of Alabama varsity, 1934, victors over Stanford in
the 1935 Rose Bowl, 29-13.

State before encountering Tennessee. "Win this game,"
Thomas told his charges, "and you'll go all the way."

Howell took the words to heart. His punting, running, and passing moved Coach Neyland to proclaim after
the Tide's thrilling victory that Howell was the greatest
back in the South.

The game was tied 6-6 in the third period when
Howell's punting kept moving the Vols backward until
Alabama was set up at the Tennessee 22. Hutson gained
six yards on the end-around, then latched onto a nine-
yard toss from Riley Smith. The end-around was called
again and Hutson knifed in for the winning score.

But the Tide had to stave off two last-minute Tennessee threats, with Howell saving one score when he
made an open-field tackle on a punt return.

Howell's finest game came when Thomas made

another declaration about the importance of a contest. It was the final game of the season, Howell's last appearance in Birmingham and Thomas pointed out that a victory was necessary if they wanted a trip to the Rose Bowl.

Vanderbilt was the opponent and Howell responded. He accounted for 318 yards rushing and returning punts. He scored two touchdowns, and when Thomas took him out of the game in the fourth period, the 28,000 fans gave him a standing ovation. Howell and the Crimson Tide were off to California.

1935: ALABAMA 29, STANFORD 13

Wrote Grantland Rice: "Dixie Howell, the human howitzer from Hartford, Ala., blasted the Rose Bowl dreams of Stanford today with one of the greatest all-around exhibitions football has ever known."

Rice might have added that Howell enjoyed one of the finest individual quarters in any football game. Howell stunned the 84,474 fans in the last 13 minutes of the second period when Alabama scored 22 points. He completed eight of nine passes, including a 67-yard scamper, scored two touchdowns, and passed 59 yards to Hutson for another.

The second-quarter blitz was called the greatest exhibition of passing in football history and it was all the more amazing because the excellent Stanford defense had yielded only two touchdowns all season.

Stanford, in fact, was so confident of its defense it could not believe Alabama was moving so easily and chose to kick off rather than receive after the Tide's first two scores.

Stanford led 7-0 when three Howell passes moved Alabama to the five, from where Howell tallied. Alabama took the ensuing kickoff, moved quickly for a Riley Smith field goal that gave it a 9-6 lead. Still Stanford was unbelieving and kicked off again. Just three plays later

Don Hutson, All-American end, 1934.

Howell roamed to his right and zipped down the sidelines 67 yards and Alabama led 16-7. Smith intercepted a pass on the Alabama 46 with only eight seconds remaining in the half. Thomas sent in conservative quarterback Tilden (Happy) Campbell with orders to run a safe play on the ground to kill the remaining seconds.

But the gambling Smith had already called a pass play before he left the huddle. Howell's sub Joe Riley was to do the throwing this time. Riley found the magnificent Hutson 24 yards downfield. Hutson gathered it in and rambled the final 30 yards for the touchdown.

Hutson caught six passes for 164 yards while Howell alone outgained Stanford, and sportswriter Mark Kelly was moved to write these words:

"Open the page once more in the Book of Football Revelations and add under these names:

Dorais to Rockne

Wyman to Bastian

Friedman to Oosterbaan, those of

HOWELL TO HUTSON

And let the last stay in capital letters because it should top the list of two-men combinations in football to make history."

Grantland Rice added: "Dixie Howell gave you the impression of Dizzy Dean throwing strikes, an antelope along the ground and one of the finest kickers the Rose Bowl has ever seen."

No one could deny Alabama its fourth national championship in nine years or Howell and Hutson their rightful place among the game's best. Both would later be inducted into Football's Hall of Fame along with their coach, Frank Thomas.

It was a mountaintop experience for the Crimson Tide but they learned quickly how the mighty can be humbled.

1935: HOWARD 7, ALABAMA 7

The 1935 season opened without Howell, Hutson, and Lee, who had graduated, and the daring Smith who was sidelined by an injury. But no one was greatly concerned because the first game was a warmup against

Alabama, however, led only 7-0 in the fourth quarter and had been held without a first down in the third period. Howard contained the Tide in its own end of the field the entire game.

Finally Howard got its break. Alabama was penalized to its own 37 for roughness. Then on third down from its 34, Howard's Harbin passed to Snell for the touchdown. The extra point was made and all Tuscaloosa was stunned by the resulting deadlock.

Things would not get a lot better that year. After beating George Washington 39-0 before 30,000 in Washington's Griffith Stadium, the Tide returned home and lost its first game in new Denny Stadium, 20-7, to Mississippi State.

The loss to State held a special meaning, however, because it was the setting that told the football world something of the inner drive and determination of Paul Bryant.

Bryant was taken out of the game in the first quarter with a broken foot. But he returned in the third quarter to finish the contest. Tennessee was the opponent next week and Bryant couldn't miss his last chance to play against the Vols.

He rode the train to Knoxville, his foot in a cast and walking on crutches. He had the cast removed the day of the game, and played until the Tide had built up a secure lead en route to a 25-0 victory. One account called it Bryant's best game.

But the season ended on a downbeat when Vanderbilt upset the fumbling Tide (five fumbles were lost) 14-6.

Vandy scored the clinching touchdown in the final seconds when a punt was fumbled in the end zone.

The 1936 Tide was unbeaten, being deadlocked only by Tennessee 0-0 but no bowls came calling to Tuscaloosa. Louisiana State won the S.E.C. title by virtue of the Alabama-Tennessee tie and went to the Sugar Bowl while Mississippi was invited to the Orange Bowl.

A spotless record appeared necessary for consideration so Thomas' 1937 outfit reeled off nine victories in a row including two thrillers in the last three weeks over Tulane and Vanderbilt. That earned the Crimson Tide a fifth Rose Bowl journey.

1937: ALABAMA 9, TULANE 6

The game was in its final minutes tied 6-6. Little Herschel Mosley got off a 51-yard punt for 'Bama to the Tulane two-yard line.

Tulane decided to punt out of trouble but Kilgrow returned it 16 yards to the 23. Four plays later Sandy Sanford tried a 32-yard field goal. It sailed just over the crossbar and Alabama won even though the play was actually illegal. Alabama had only six men on the scrimmage line but the violation went undetected by the officials.

1937: ALABAMA 9, VANDERBILT 7

Sanford repeated the heroics 19 days later on Dudley Field in Nashville against Vanderbilt to secure the Rose Bowl trip. Vanderbilt led 7-6 with six minutes left in the game. Vandy had just stalled a 75-yard Alabama push at its own five-yard line but was forced to punt back to the Crimson Tide. Mosley passed 31 yards to Kilgrow then hit Vic Bradford for 18. Then from an acute angle at the 27, Sanford punched over the winning field goal.

1938: CALIFORNIA 13, ALABAMA 0

From a standpoint of quality talent this was not one of

University of Alabama varsity, 1937.

Frank Thomas' great teams. But he had squeezed out every ounce of productivity in it and had won games when his team had been outplayed. It was generally conceded Thomas had done a brilliant coaching job to bring it through undefeated.

But on this New Year's Day no amount of coaching genius could help against a rugged California team that despite its 6-4 record was deep in talented athletes including Quarterback Johnny (Jelly Belly) Meek, devastating blocking end Perry Schwartz, halfback Sam Chapman, destined to be a major league outfielder, 215-pound center Bob Herwig and guard Vard Stockton. There was also a junior tailback named Vic Bottari whom the Tide could not reckon with that day. He scored both touchdowns on end runs of three and five yards climaxing long drives.

Still Alabama came close. The Tide drove to the six-yard line and the one only to lose the ball on fumbles. Two other fumbles were lost and four times California intercepted passes.

Thomas recognized California's superiority:

"The most powerful team we've met since Bobby Grayson's Stanford team in 1935. We've played some tough ones these last two years but those Bears kept socking with all their might . . . my ball club played to the limit of its capablities but I guess California was just too good."

If Thomas felt his team had started out the year by losing some prestige on the West Coast it was quick to regain it.

1938: ALABAMA 19, SOUTHERN CALIFORNIA 7

The Crimson Tide was scheduled to open the season

1938 Rose Bowl—California halfback Sam Chapman (48) kicks a point after touchdown. California won, 13-0.

at the Los Angeles Coliseum against the U.S.C. Trojans. Mosley passed for two touchdowns in the second quarter, one to Bill Slemmons and the other to Gene Blackwell, who made a leaping one-handed grab ending an 80-yard march.

Hal Hughes intercepted a Trojan pass and ran it in for another score in the fourth period giving the Tide a 19-0 lead and the shutout was ruined only by an Alabama fumble at its own one-yard line, which U.S.C. recovered and converted into its only touchdown. Thomas called it "one of our finest victories."

The season was marred by a 13-0 loss to a fine Tennessee team three weeks later but Alabama provided some

Alabama-Southern California, 1938. Alabama halfback George Zivich (11) gains 10 yards in first-quarter action. U.S.C. defenders are Boyd Morgan (attempting the tackle), Ray George (28) and Bob Hoffman (45). Player on his back at right is Herschel Mosley. Alabama won, 19-7.

thrills for its followers in the final three weeks of the season. The streak of close calls began on November 5th when Vic Bradford kicked a field goal as time was running out on fourth down from Tulane's nine-yard line to earn a 3-0 victory. Tulane had stopped previous Alabama drives at its 2, 5, 10, and 15 yard lines while never getting any closer to the Tide goal line than the 46.

Georgia Tech led 14-7 in the final period when Charles Boswell, later famous as a blind golfer, received a Tech punt at the Alabama 34. On the first play, he flipped a short pass to Bradford, who tossed back to Alvin Davis. Davis raced more than 50 yards for the score. Georgia Tech coaches protested the play was illegal but to no avail, and the game ended 14-14.

Finally, against Vanderbilt, the Tide generated a 72-yard march late in the third period. Bradford scored from the two on the first play of the fourth quarter and the Crimson Tide registered another squeaker 7-0 to end the season with a 7-1-1 record.

1939: ALABAMA 7, FORDHAM 6

The year 1939 marked the first time in ten years the Tide had lost three games. But the 5-3-1 record had one highly satisfying moment. It came on October 7 in the Polo Grounds against the Fordham Rams and the Seven Blocks of Granite. Boswell and Jimmy Nelson inspired the 7-6 victory for the visitors.

The Tide scored early on a 62-yard drive that culminated when Boswell faked a handoff to John Hanson and gave the ball instead to Nelson who circled 13 yards for the touchdown. Sandy Sanford's extra point would prove to be decisive. Fordham finally tallied in the fourth period after the Rams blocked a quick kick and recovered the ball on Alabama's 17. The extra point·was missed and the Tide had its upset.

14

"The War Babies"

They called it the "Fighting Forties" and the decade brought war, which profoundly affected everything including the sport of football. Alabama lost its able-bodied men to the service, had to disband its team in 1943 and played with a team of freshmen and those unfit physically for combat in 1944. That was the beginning of Coach Frank Thomas' "War Babies" and it became his most beloved team.

Still Alabama went to five bowl games and four in a row including their last visit to Pasadena in 1946. 'Bama won the Southeastern championship in 1945 with its only undefeated team of the decade. The Crimson Tide even played its first night game on September 27, 1940, beating Spring Hill College 26-0 before 7,500 fans at Murphy High School Stadium in Mobile, Alabama.

It was a period of unusual happenings and few were more weird than the 1942 Cotton Bowl which proved, if nothing else, that the only statistic that really matters is the number of points on the scoreboard.

1942: ALABAMA 29, TEXAS A. & M. 21

Texas A. & M. held the Crimson Tide to just one first down, one pass completion in 13 attempts, only 32 offensive plays and just 75 yards net offense.

The Aggies in turn rattled off 79 plays, recorded 13 first downs, gained 309 yards rushing and passing and completed 13 of 42 passes. They were penalized only five yards while 81 yards in penalties were marched off against the Tide.

Thus it seemed impossible that Alabama was leading 29-7 with only seven minutes left in the game. That was the exact circumstance, however, and it could be traced directly to the fact that the Aggies had suffered seven interceptions and lost five fumbles to the ball-hawking Crimson Tide.

The shocking reversal which defied the Aggies' statistical dominance began in the third quarter with the score tied 7-7.

Jimmy Nelson, an All-S.E.C. halfback, started it when he returned a punt 72 yards for a touchdown. Minutes later Joe Sharpe recovered a fumble at the A. & M. 21 and Nelson scored on the next play.

An interception set up George Hecht's field goal in the fourth quarter, then All-S.E.C. end Holt Rast picked off a Derance Moser pass and went ten yards for the final Alabama touchdown.

The remainder of the game was dominated by the Aggies, who scored twice more, but it was too late to compensate for the alertness of the opportunistic Tide.

1942: GEORGIA 21, ALABAMA 10

The war was now having its influence on the colleges.

Holt Rast, All-American end, 1941.

Many were forced to drop football in 1942 and the best athletes were enrolling at service academies, pre-flight schools, and other institutions set up to feed the war effort.

Alabama had a pair of All-American linemen itself and wasn't yet ready to put its football uniforms in mothballs. Led by center Joe Domnanovich and tackle Don Whitmire, the Crimson Tide won its first five games before the first of three losses to Georgia schools.

The University of Georgia's Frank Sinkwich, an All-American quarterback, rallied the Bulldogs from a 10-0 deficit with two fourth-quarter touchdown passes to end George Poschner, who later would be decorated for gallantry in the war, and Alabama suffered a 21-10 loss.

Two weeks later Georgia Tech scored in the first period and held on to shut out Alabama 7-0. In the final game of the season the Tide tackled the Georgia Pre-

Joe Domnanovich,
All-American center
and team captain, 1942.

Flight Skycrackers, a team filled with former all-star names such as Suffridge, Whitlow, Lumpkin, Foxx, Filchock, Blandin, and Hickerson. Hank Crisp, the line coach at Alabama, was a civilian trainer at the army base in Athens, Georgia, and was one of the coaches for the Skycrackers.

The collection of soldier-athletes smashed 'Bama 35-19. The Crimson Tide was unable to get a touchdown until the final period.

Despite its 7-3 record, Alabama was invited to meet eastern power Boston College in the Orange Bowl New Year's Day and for the first few minutes the Tide thought Georgia Pre-Flight had flown in to demolish them again.

1943: ALABAMA 37, BOSTON COLLEGE 21

Mike Holovak was the scourge of the Tide in the early moments. He raced 65 yards for a touchdown on

Boston College's third play and minutes later wiggled free on a 35-yard touchdown jaunt around left end.

Domnanovich, Alabama's captain and All-American center, summoned his teammates to a huddle prior to the next kickoff.

"Don't give up," he charged them. "We haven't had a chance to go with the ball yet. We're going to receive and we're going to run them into the ground."

From that point the Tide took command. It rolled 60 yards for a touchdown that came early in the second quarter on a 15-yard pass from Russ Mosley to Wheeler Leeth.

On the ensuing kickoff B.C. fumbled and Don Salls recovered on the 33. Four plays later Johnny August passed 17 yards to Ted Cook for the score.

The Eagles couldn't move against the Alabama defense, which forced another punt and shortly afterward Bobby Tom Jenkins broke loose on a 40-yard scoring scamper. 'Bama led 19-14.

The Eagles had one last fling before the half. Fullback Carl Lucas passed 45 yards to Holovak, who eventually scored on a 2-yard plunge giving Boston College a 21-19 lead. Hecht, however, kicked a field goal from the 15-yard line with 30 seconds remaining before halftime. Alabama finally had a lead that it would keep.

That was the last of Alabama football until September 30, 1944, when Thomas trotted out his "War Babies" into the Tigers' den at Louisiana State University before 32,000 screaming fans in Baton Rouge.

These players gave the most with the least and won the heart of Thomas and Alabama followers. They were ends Ralph Jones, John McConville, and Billy Fields; tackles Tom Whitley, Buddy Edwards, and Francis Cassidy; guards John Wozniak, Jack Green, Bruno Fillipine, and William Conway; center Vaughn Mancha; and backs Hal Self, Lowell Tew, Norwood Hodges, Hugh

Frank W. Thomas, coach
of the Alabama
"War Babies".

Morrow, Fred Grant, George Albright, James Roberts, and John Wade.

Oh, yes, and there was also a skinny little 18-year-old kid with an ulcer from Birmingham's Woodlawn High School who didn't even want to go to college.

He weighed only 155 pounds, but he had an amazingly strong and accurate right arm and a style of throwing a football that more than compensated for his small stature. His name was Harry Gilmer. He made the jump pass famous and even in high school was touted by Zipp Newman as being "as fine a passer as there is in football. This goes for the pros."

Gilmer, however, only wanted to "get a job and get married" after he left high school, but Thomas finally lured him to Tuscaloosa by adding Gilmer's high school coach, Malcom Laney, to his staff of assistants.

1944: L.S.U. 27, ALABAMA 27

And so the freshman-dominated Crimson Tide went back to the football wars and established immediately that this particular team had plenty of character as well as a brilliant field leader in Gilmer.

Its first test was at L.S.U. and the Tigers were considered at least a one-touchdown favorite. They started out as if that margin was a conservative estimate when L.S.U.'s Rowan raced 64 yards for a touchdown. L.S.U. also had a great quarterback in Y.A. Tittle, who would go on to fame in the pros, but despite the talent and fast start, the Tigers found themselves trailing Alabama 27-21 in the fourth quarter. Gilmer had scored on runs of 95 yards (on a kickoff return) and 23 yards and set up two other scores with his passing.

But L.S.U. blocked a Gilmer punt and recovered it in the end zone in the fourth quarter to create a 27-27 tie. The extra point failed and the Tide escaped with an impressive draw.

There was also a scoreless tie with Tennessee and a 14-7 upset loss to Georgia, who scored in the final period for the victory. Still Alabama was an attractive and exciting team and the Sugar Bowl wanted the Tide in a matchup against Duke, a powerful team supplemented by navy trainees.

1945: DUKE 29, ALABAMA 26

One account of this battle called it "the most sensational, thrilling and spectacular exhibition of gridiron warfare not only in the history of the Sugar Bowl but in the annals of all of the other bowl games combined."

Perhaps it was an exaggeration but it was a remarkable spectacle. Its entertainment value was heightened by the atmosphere of the day when the heartbreak of war was trying to be forgotten for a moment by a crowd of 72,000 dominated by soldiers, sailors, airmen, and marines in uniform, many of whom had just returned from battle.

It was a dramatic event and little Harry Gilmer was the star, even in defeat. He was so sensational, in fact, that the Duke players, led by the great Tom Davis, mobbed the tailback when the final gun was sounded as a tribute to his play.

Gilmer completed all eight of his tosses, most of them difficult scrambling jump passes. In one instance that was typical, Gilmer was blitzed. He tripped over one tackler but maintained his balance, slithered out of the grasp of two more Blue Devils and, while on the run, vaulted into the air and fired an arrow 41 yards right on target to end Ralph Jones.

Duke had scored on its first series when halfback George Clark burst loose for 52 yards, then scampered into the end zone from the 14.

But Gilmer's passing produced three consecutive touchdowns and a 19-7 lead before Davis narrowed the lead to 19-13 at halftime.

Davis then rattled off ten consecutive carries in the third quarter to personally account for a 64-yard touchdown drive and the Blue Devils recaptured the lead 20-19.

Alabama's Hugh Morrow picked off a pass by Cliff Lewis and sprinted 75 yards, putting the Tide back in front but the lead was destined to change for the fourth time.

The Blue Devils ground relentlessly downfield before being halted at the Tide 1-yard line with three minutes left.

Thomas decided the most prudent way to get out of the tight situation was to take a deliberate safety, then have a free punt from the 20. John Wade punted to the Duke 40 but Clark spun free on a 20-yard return. Jim LaRue swept 20 yards on a reverse. Then Clark covered the final 20 yards, carrying two Alabama tacklers the last 7.

There was time for one last play. Gilmer hurled a long pass which Jones snared, eluded all but one Duke tackler who made a diving effort and tripped Jones by latching onto one foot as time expired.

Grantland Rice said he'd "never seen a more thrilling game" and the "War Babies" had been so sensational the team held a "victory" party in New Orleans that night.

1945: ALABAMA 27, GEORGIA 14

One of the most memorable confrontations of two exceptional football stars took place on October 27, 1945, in Birmingham before 26,000 who were treated to a duel between Georgia's magnificent Charlie Trippi and Gilmer.

Neither Trippi nor Gilmer disappointed anyone. They punted, passed and ran brilliantly, and each produced a spectacular play.

Trippi had been discharged from the service just two weeks earlier and had not had sufficient time to learn the Bulldogs' T-formation attack. But it didn't seem to bother him. On one play he faked a pass, then skirted end, and weaved 31 yards for a touchdown, breaking three tackles en route. He also had a 65-yard touchdown pass to Moseley before being forced out of the game because of an injury in the fourth quarter. He was accorded a standing ovation by the Birmingham fans as he left.

Gilmer completed thirteen of nineteen passes for 121 yards, three for touchdowns and intercepted one of Trippi's tosses. He threw a 13-yard scoring pass to Hugh Morrow, a 12-yard touchdown to Norwood Hodges and, with three Georgia defenders hanging on him, managed a leaping nine-yard touchdown pass to Fred Grant.

A week later Gilmer gained 216 yards in only six car-

1946 Rose Bowl—The Alabama backfield, from left: Lowell Tew, Norwood Hodges, Hal Self, and Harry Gilmer. Alabama beat Southern California, 34-14.

ries, completed his only two passes for 50 yards, had touchdown runs of 95 and 59 yards and led the Tide to a 60-19 thumping of Kentucky.

Gilmer wasn't the only star for Alabama. There was All-American Vaughn Mancha, and among the other leaders was Lowell Tew, a 195-pound halfback who was an excellent runner, pass receiver, and blocker. Tew was outstanding throughout the Tide's perfect season, its last for sixteen years. Alabama wasn't challenged in the remaining games, scoring at least 55 points in each of its last four contests to win the Southeastern Conference with ease. It was the highest scoring team Alabama had produced, accumulating 430 points.

1946 Rose Bowl—Alabama's Harry Gilmer (52) cracks through to the Southern Cal 1-yard line, setting up Alabama's first touchdown in the first quarter. Alabama won, 34-14.

1946: ALABAMA 34, SOUTHERN CALIFORNIA 14

Alabama was favored in the Rose Bowl but West Coast fans remained skeptical despite the Crimson Tide's previous victories at Pasadena. By the third period Alabama led 27-0, and the 93,000 fans were convinced of the Crimson Tide's abilities because they were now watching the reserves pound away at the Trojans, who had won eight consecutive Rose Bowls dating back to 1923.

Alabama ran up 351 yards total offense to just 41 for Southern Cal including just six by rushing. And Harry

Alabama's starting lineup for the 1948 Sugar Bowl game against Texas.
Line, from left: Jim Cain, RE; Dick Flowers, RT; Ray Richeson, RG; Vaughn
Mancha, C; John Wozniak, LG; Tom Whitley, LT; Rebel Steiner, LE.

Gilmer took it relatively easy against the Trojans, throwing only eleven times for one touchdown but gaining 116 yards in sixteen rushes. Hal Self caught Gilmer's 24-yard touchdown pass and scored another on a quarterback sneak. Tew and Hodges also collected touchdowns and the South's last representative in the Rose Bowl earned an impressive 34-14 victory. It was also the last bowl game for the ailing Thomas, who was forced out of coaching in 1947 and died seven years later.

Red Drew assumed the coaching duties from Thomas in 1947, the final "War Babies" season, and took the Tide bowling again although the outcome wasn't pleasant.

Drew's start was not a happy one either. After beating Mississippi Southern 34-7 the Tide was upset by Tulane, which scored all its points in a 3-minute span for a 21-20

Backfield, from left: Bill Cadenhead, RHB; Lowell Tew, FB;
Hugh Morrow, QB; Harry Gilmer, LHB.

victory.

But the Tide rebounded after the Tulane setback and on November 22 took a 6-2 record and hopes for a Sugar Bowl bid into the battle against Louisiana State that would match Gilmer against the Tigers' Quarterback Y.A. Tittle.

In the opening minutes of the game, Gilmer returned a punt 92 yards for a touchdown and the Tide rolled on to a 41-12 victory, defeated Miami (Fla.) 21-6 a week later and was matched against Texas in the Sugar Bowl.

1948: TEXAS 27, ALABAMA 7

Gilmer had usually been the victor in confrontations with other greats of the day such as Tittle and Trippi. But in Dallas this day a Longhorn quarterback named Bobby Layne bested him.

Layne scored once and passed for another in the second half to dissolve a 7-7 tie. He completed 10 of 24 passes for 183 yards.

Meanwhile Gilmer suffered what he admitted was the worst day in his college career. He completed only 3 of 11 passes and gained just 6 yards rushing. One of his passes was intercepted and returned for a touchdown. He fumbled at his own 5, setting up another Texas score. Gilmer did, however, pass for the Tide's only touchdown but his final game in the Crimson colors was hardly typical.

The Roller Coaster

If there were two games that symbolized the turbulent heights and depths of Alabama's football fortunes in the 1950s they were Red Drew's last two post-season appearances—the 1953 Orange Bowl and the 1954 Cotton Bowl. They demonstrated, if nothing else, how abruptly fortune can change.

After attracting no bowl bids with a 9-2 record in 1950 when All-American halfback Ed Salem, end Al Lary, guard Mike Mizerany, and center Pat O'Sullivan formed the core of a good team, the Crimson Tide slipped to a 5-6 mark in 1951, its first losing season since 1903.

But the Tide rebounded in 1952. Bobby Marlow rushed for 950 yards in 176 carries, Clell Hobson passed and ran for more than 1,000 yards joining Howell, Gilmer, and Salem in that category, and Cecil (Hootie) Ingram led a tight defense by intercepting ten passes.

The season began with four consecutive victories before Alabama was stopped cold by Tennessee, the No. 1

defensive team in the nation, 20-0 at Knoxville. Three more victories followed, then Georgia Tech edged the Crimson Tide 7-3. A 27-7 thumping of Maryland and 21-0 shutout of Auburn, however, convinced the Orange Bowl officials that Alabama would be an attractive team to debut with Syracuse in the first national telecast of bowl games.

1953: ALABAMA 61, SYRACUSE 6

It was the most one-sided contest in bowl history. Drew used all 46 of his players and still complained that "I couldn't stop them."

Hobson was the primary culprit. He completed 14 of 22 passes for 207 yards including eight to end Joe Curtis. There were eighteen Orange Bowl records set, among them the Tide's 586 yards of total offense and the 818 yards amassed by both teams.

Alabama led only 7-6 in the second quarter on Hobson's 27-yard pass to Bobby Luna. But quickly Marlow scored and Corky Tharp took a 50-yard pass from Hobson to create a 21-6 halftime lead.

Six touchdowns followed in the second half.

By the third quarter the Orange Bowl was rapidly emptying because many of the 66,280 fans wanted to watch the other bowl games on television. And bowl officials were pleading with the timekeeper to speed up the game so that the contest would not be preempted by the network before its completion.

The 1953 season was one of the strangest any Southeastern Conference champion ever experienced. Alabama won the title and a trip to the Cotton Bowl even though it was upset in the opening game by Mississippi Southern and suffered three ties in conference games against Louisiana State, Tennessee, and Mississippi State. The Tide also lost to national champion Maryland 21-0 but managed not to lose any conference games and was able to

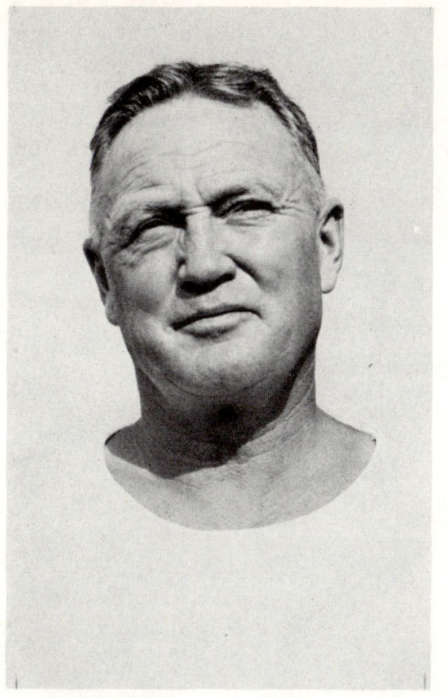

Harold D. (Red) Drew in 1948.

sneak in the back door to steal the crown.

The bowl bid came down to the traditional last game against Auburn and, as usual, it wasn't easy. Auburn had a good team, led by Fob James and Vince Dooley, and the Tigers jumped out to an early 7-0 lead. Alabama scrambled for a tie on Rocky Stone's 14-yard run and it appeared the Tide was headed for a fourth tie in the conference. But Bobby Luna kicked a field goal in the final moments to earn the 10-7 victory.

1954: RICE 28, ALABAMA 6

It was the second period of the Cotton Bowl and Rice led 7-6 on a 76-yard touchdown run by All-American halfback Dicky Moegle. Rice was in possession of the ball at its own 5-yard line when Moegle took the handoff and sprinted around right end. The Owls' interference leveled Crimson Tide tacklers and suddenly Moegle was wide

Tommy Lewis (42) walks off the field at halftime in the
1954 Cotton Bowl game against Rice. At left is Rice end Lamoine Holland;
at right is Rice center Leo Rucka.

open racing down the right sideline. There was no tackler within five yards of him and no one was gaining on the sprinter who would score three times this day and gain 265 yards in eleven carries.

Something happened then so swiftly that viewers began to doubt what they thought they saw. Moegle was down at the Alabama 41-yard line and it appeared that someone from the Alabama bench had darted out and tackled him.

That was precisely what occurred. Halfback Tommy Lewis, who had scored Alabama's touchdown earlier, had left the bench and—bareheaded—tackled Moegle. Referee Cliff Shaw ruled Moegle would have scored and gave him a 95-yard touchdown run. Even Coach Drew conceded Moegle "probably would have made the touchdown anyway."

Lewis was crushed.

"I'm too emotional," he said afterward. "I kept telling myself, 'I didn't do it. I didn't do it.' But I knew I had.

"I'm just too full of 'Bama. He just ran too close. I know I'll be hearing about this for the rest of my life."

The next day the *Dallas Morning News* ran a front page editorial written by Managing Editor Felix R. McKnight, a former sportswriter. It said, in part:

"Tommy Lewis, a genuine competitor even while on the bench, had committed a forgivable error that will live with him forever. He quickly and abjectly apologized to Moegle and the Rice team and he did it three more times, finally, at game's end walking out of the big stadium with his arm around Moegle.

"Texans know competitive spirit. We thrive on it.

"He's quite a fighter—and we like them that way in Texas."

The embarrassing Cotton Bowl, however, was a signal for football's most disastrous decline at Alabama. The Tide lost its opener again in 1954 to Mississippi Southern 7-2, scored only 14 points in its last six games and finished with a 4-5-2 record. There wouldn't be another winning season until Paul Bryant arrived in 1958 and after Auburn trounced the Tide 28-0 to end the '54 season, Red Drew resigned.

J. B. (Ears) Whitworth replaced Drew with a three-year contract in 1955 and utter failure set in at the Capstone. The Tide was 0-10 under Whitworth the first year and the only noteworthy event came when it won for the first time in 21 games on Oct. 27, 1956, beating Mississippi State 13-12. There was nothing redeeming about Whitworth's record. He had lost all three meetings decisively to the two primary rivals, Tennessee and Auburn. That alone would be enough for dismissal even if he'd won the others. But Whitworth managed just four victories in three years. There were no All-Americans, not even a first team Southeastern Conference star off the Alabama squads.

1958: L.S.U. 13, ALABAMA 3

It was September 27, the scene was Ladd Stadium in Mobile, and Paul (Bear) Bryant was making his debut as head coach at his alma mater. The opposition, L.S.U., was to become national champions for the first time that season, led by its All-American back Billy Cannon, quarterback Warren Rabb and Johnny Robinson.

Bryant's first team wasn't blessed with abundant talent. In fact, several of the most promising recruits had quit the team either in spring practice the previous March or in the fall. His players always denied Bryant was brutal in the workouts. The coach only demanded of his charges what he demanded of himself—"hard work." He often said "I'm just an ordinary coach who works hard."

And he wanted to find out which players would be dependable once the game started. "If they're quitters, I want them to quit in practice, not in a game. There's been enough of that," he said. Therefore he demanded "all they have" in practice.

What Bryant came up with was a lightweight, scrappy collection of athletes who held the same devotion to the sport as did their coach. It included a 150-pound halfback, Marlin (Scooter) Dyess and two guards who weighed only 190 pounds.

Louisiana State was an overwhelming favorite but not an overwhelming winner. Bryant established immediately that nothing would come easily for the enemy.

In the second quarter Cannon was given a fierce jolt, the ball popped into the air and Alabama's Duff Morrison picked it off on the run and wasn't hauled down until he reached the L.S.U. 4-yard line. It was a 45-yard run but the Crimson Tide simply couldn't negotiate those final 4 yards with its limited offense against L.S.U.'s famed "Chinese Bandits" defense and had to settle for a field goal.

Still the Tide had a 3-0 lead, which none of the 34,000 had really expected. And Bryant's boys made the Tigers work for the lead they finally gained in the third quarter. L.S.U. ground out a 67-yard march that ended on a Rabb-to-Robinson touchdown pass of 9 yards. Quick kicks of 55 and 52 yards by Dyess kept the Tigers stymied until the fourth quarter when Cannon wiggled free for an 11-yard run.

It was one of the closest calls L.S.U. would experience all season. Coach Paul Dietzel's Tigers were destined to finish as the only college team in the nation with a perfect record and were named the sports team of the year.

Already there was a hint of things to come at Alabama.

1958: ALABAMA 17, GEORGIA TECH 8

Entering this game in Atlanta on November 15, the season had been a bitter struggle for the Tide. After the L.S.U. loss there had been a scoreless tie with Vanderbilt, a 29-6 victory over Furman—Bryant's first as Alabama's head coach—and a 14-7 setback against Tennessee. Mississippi State (9-7) and Georgia (12-0) had fallen before Tulane upended the Tide 13-7 in New Orleans. The record was 3-3-1 which wasn't bad, most alumni rationalized, considering their team had won just four games in the three previous years and Bryant was having to rebuild from the wreckage left by Whitworth.

There had been reasons for optimism along the way but the first concrete evidence came on this day when Georgia Tech, the most formidable of the Tide's five victims in 1958 and a two-touchdown favorite, fell in their own stadium on homecoming day.

Memphis State bowed the following Saturday 14-0.

Then came Auburn's fifth consecutive victory over Alabama 14-8. The only consolation was that at least this one was close and the Tide almost salvaged victory. Dyess scored on a 9-yard run, Gary O'Steen passed to Bobby Jackson for the 2-point conversion then a last-second pass to Jerry Spruiell·was just tipped away at the goal line. Auburn fans would be forced to remember this game because the Tigers would not score on the Crimson Tide the next four years.

1959: ALABAMA 9, GEORGIA TECH 7

Georgia Tech was bound for a Gator Bowl appearance against Arkansas while Alabama, suddenly not losing any more, was thinking bowl too. The Tide had lost its opening game to Georgia 17-3 and the Bulldogs, led by elusive quarterback Fran Tarkenton, were destined to win the Southeastern Conference and beat Missouri in the Orange Bowl.

After Georgia, however, Alabama managed to go through six games unbeaten with only 7-7 ties against Tennessee and Vanderbilt spoiling the record. It was a heady feeling finally renewed for 'Bama fans by Bryant. Everyone realized now that the most formidable opponent left was Georgia Tech.

When the Tech victory was achieved, Alabama backers cautiously began to wonder about a bowl. There were two hurdles left. Memphis State fell 14-7. Finally there was Auburn. Tommy Brooker booted a 27-yard field goal in the first half and early in the third quarter Bobby Skelton flipped a short pass to Dyess, who raced 39 yards for the clincher.

Alabama had a 10-0 victory, a 7-1-2 record and the happy sound of the telephone ringing from bowl officials was heard in Tuscaloosa for the first time in six years. It would ring for 15 consecutive seasons through December 31, 1973.

1959: PENN STATE 7, ALABAMA 0

They had to create a new bowl, the seventh post season contest for major college teams, in order to get Alabama back into the bowl business but that didn't matter to Bryant. It was important only that the practice be renewed.

There were only 36,000 freezing fans rattling around in 100,000-seat Philadelphia Stadium, attracted to the Liberty Bowl, the first bowl attempted in cold-weather country. (It would later yield to the weather and financial freeze, moving to Memphis, Tennessee). If Alabama found the weather uncomfortable it didn't find the opponent any more soothing. Liberty Bowl officials had picked Penn State and Coach Rip Engle's Nittany Lions had fashioned an 8-2 record that included a narrow 20-18 loss to National Champion Syracuse.

The Nittany Lions were armed with talent. Quarterback Richie Lucas was the most troublesome but there was also sophomore halfback Roger Kochman and another quarterback, Galen Hall, who would do the most damage to the Crimson Tide.

The cold and high winds made offense almost impossible—at least the conventional attack. The Crimson Tide only once penetrated as far as the enemy 28-yard line.

Penn State had done better, reaching the Tide 1, 5, and 8-yard lines in first-half drives that were repulsed.

Again the Tide seemed to have halted a Nittany Lion march with time running out in the first half. The ball was at the 18-yard line, second down and 6. Without huddling, Penn State went into a field-goal formation. Hall knelt for the snap and Sam Stellatella stood behind him prepared to kick.

Hall, however, took the snap, rolled to his right and threw back to the left. It was a screen pass to Kochman who scooted 20 yards, stumbling over the final 3 to score the game's only touchdown.

Penn State outgained Alabama 319 yards to 131, had eighteen first downs to eight for the Tide and Bryant agreed the outcome could have been much more one-sided.

But Bryant had brought his alma mater back a long way in two short years. Alabama had been reestablished as a football team that no one could ignore. The reputation of the many glory years was being revived, retooled, and brought up to date.

The 1950s, which had contained Alabama's most painful Saturdays, were ending with a basis for legitimate optimism.

16

"Team of the Decade"

Like a giant crimson machine, precision programmed to near perfection, Alabama began turning out an assembly line of remarkable football teams in the 1960s. Neither the yearly attrition through graduation, depletion because of injury, nor the suggestion of scandal could interrupt the flow.

They were minting All-Americans, particularly quarterbacks, in astonishing numbers and the plant foreman at Tuscaloosa, Paul Bryant, kept a close quality check to insure that not one particle of the valuable material was wasted.

The end product was victories, the astonishing total of 90 in the ten-year period. Alabama lost only sixteen and tied four during the 1960s, the best record of any collegiate team. There were 20 All-Americans, 33 All-Southeastern Conference selections, a bowl trip every year, four conference titles, and three national championships.

Bryant had an exceptional quarterback virtually ev-

Assistant Coach Howard Schnellenberger (second from left) and members of the 1964 Tide varsity show off their No. 1 plaque from 1961 and hold fingers up to show that Alabama is No. 1 again. Players are, from left: Dan Kearley, Jimmy Fuller, Steve Bowman, and Wayne Trimble.

ery year. First came gutty Pat Trammell, an All-American in 1961, followed by the flamboyant Joe Namath. Next was Steve Sloan, an All-American selection in 1965. Lefty Kenny Stabler was the 1967 All-American selection, and finally Scott Hunter.

Bryant's teams simply would not be beaten even when all conditions pointed to defeat. His 1961, 1964, and 1965 productions were voted best in the nation and Bryant protested that his unbeaten 1966 outfit that clobbered Nebraska 34-7 in the Sugar Bowl also should have been accorded the honor. Notre Dame, which settled for a 10-10 tie with Michigan State, was named the 1966 champion instead.

Of his national championship teams, Bryant said:

"They reached the pinnacle for two reasons. One, each of those teams had its share of outstanding football players. Two, all of them showed that willingness to do what had to be done ... they had mental toughness ... you've got to be convinced that the fourth quarter belongs to you."

An excellent example of Bryant's preaching in action came November 12, 1960, in Atlanta against Georgia Tech.

1960: ALABAMA 16, GEORGIA TECH 15

The Ramblin' Wreck would wind up the afternoon resembling their nickname, but they cruised into the locker room at halftime like a Cadillac, sporting a 15-0 lead. They had dominated the Crimson Tide in every aspect of the game. Alabama had managed just one first down—on the last play of the half.

Bryant said he told his charges nothing during intermission. If his gospel of mental toughness had not been received during the long hours on the practice field, it wasn't going to be suddenly accepted now in the eighth game of the season. Bryant was fairly confident his players were prepared for a comeback. He knew them well.

In the third quarter, quarterbacks Trammell and Bobby Skelton led the rally, directing the offense. Leon Fuller scored 'Bama's first touchdown and entering the final 15 minutes Alabama trailed 15-6.

Another drive was mounted and Skelton completed it with an 8-yard touchdown pass to Norbie Ronsonet. The extra point cut the margin to 15-13. Time was running out but the Crimson Tide defense quickly stopped Tech. Skelton was back at the throttle of the offense and moved to the Georgia Tech 14-yard line.

There were no time outs remaining for 'Bama, the

final seconds were ticking off the Grant Field clock and Richard O'Dell, an end who had never attempted a field goal, was asked to try his foot at kicking as his teammates scurried up to the scrimmage line. Skelton took the hurried snap, placed the ball down and O'Dell kicked. The ball wobbled, floated, dropped, and just cleared the back of the crossbar. The scoreboard showed that time had expired and so had a stadium full of Georgia Tech fans.

1960: ALABAMA 3, TEXAS 3

The Bluebonnet Bowl was a forum for Lee Roy Jordan, a young country lad from Excel, Alabama. Jordan was a standout in the Alabama defense that effectively shut off the Longhorns, holding them scoreless until the final 4 minutes of the game.

Alabama led 3-0 on Tommy Brooker's third-period field goal of 30 yards but the Longhorns, on one of their infrequent threats, pushed to the Alabama 3-yard line for a first down. Three plays later third-string tackle Dan Petty booted a field goal from the 10.

The Crimson Tide felt it should have won. Bobby Skelton argued he had scored from the 3-yard line in the first quarter ("I had chalk on my jersey from the goal line when I got up," Skelton insisted). But the officials ruled he had been stopped short. On the next play, fourth down, the Longhorns stopped fullback Bobby Richardson an inch short of the goal.

During 1961, however, the Crimson Tide would not be stopped short of any goal. Bryant's charges swept to 10 consecutive victories, shut out the last five opponents, captured the national championship and defeated Arkansas in the Sugar Bowl 10-3. It was, according to Zipp Newman, the best coaching job of Bryant's career for which he was appropriately honored as the Coach of the Year. He also had help from some talented and dedicated athletes led by Neighbors, Trammell, Jordan, and Fracchia.

Alabama rated as the finest defensive team in the nation. It was also a team that grew in stature as the season progressed. The most significant game on the schedule was against Georgia Tech in Birmingham on November 18. It was the game that Bryant said "convinced me they are a great team." It was also the afternoon in which the one ugly incident of the season occurred.

1961: ALABAMA 10, GEORGIA TECH 0

Fracchia pounded 16 yards for a touchdown in the second quarter, Tim Davis kicked a 32-yard field goal, and the Alabama defense held Tech to only 96 yards total offense including 30 yards on the ground. That would have made it a simple game if it had not been an episode late in the contest in which Tech halfback Chick Granning suffered severe facial injuries when struck with an elbow by Darwin Holt, Alabama linebacker. Georgia Tech officials insisted the blow appeared to be intentional, but neither the Southeastern Conference nor Alabama felt disciplinary action was necessary.

1962: ALABAMA 10, ARKANSAS 3

The Alabama defense convinced a capacity crowd in the Sugar Bowl of its superiority against a talented Razorback team that included elusive Lance Alworth, who almost latched on to a long pass in the closing moments to create a tie. The Tide held Arkansas to 55 yards passing and 113 rushing while Fracchia alone outgained the Razorbacks on the ground with 123 yards in 20 carries.

Fracchia made a twisting, turning, sidestepping 43-yard run off right tackle to the Arkansas 12-yard line from where Trammell carried in for the score on the next play in the first period. Tim Davis missed a field goal try from the 18 midway in the second period but a few minutes later he connected following a pass interception that gave

'Bama the ball at the Arkansas 20.

Trammell tried two passes into the end zone that were knocked away but Davis booted one through from the 23 and the Alabama defense did the rest, yielding only a third-quarter field goal by Mickey Gissell of 23 yards.

1962: ALABAMA 35, GEORGIA 0

This would have been a very forgettable football game (aside from the fact that it marked sophomore quarterback Joe Namath's college debut) if it had not been for a series of charges that emerged early in 1963 alleging that Bryant and Wally Butts, then athletic director at Georgia, had conspired to rig the game.

Butts was accused of divulging vital team secrets via telephone to Bryant but the charges were never proved and both Bryant and Butts won libel settlements over the matter.

Alabama entered the game as a 17-point favorite and it was doubtful if the Crimson Tide needed any information on Georgia to handle the Bulldogs with ease.

The charges, plus the fact that blacks were suing for entrance into the University of Alabama made 1962 and 1963 restless years for everyone connected with the Tuscaloosa campus.

But it didn't seem to bother Bryant's team. It rolled to a 9-1 record during the 1962 regular season, losing only to third-ranked Georgia Tech in Atlanta on November 17.

1962: GEORGIA TECH 7, ALABAMA 6

The nation's longest unbeaten streak came to an end at 26 games on this day before 53,000 in Grant Field. Georgia Tech completely dominated the first half but the Yellow Jackets' only touchdown was set up in the second period when Mike McNames intercepted a Joe Namath pass and returned it 26 yards. McNames scored moments later on a 9-yard run up the middle and Billy Lothridge's

Alabama center Lee Roy Jordan poses with quarterbacks Joe Namath (left) and Jack Hurlbut in practice before meeting Oklahoma in the Orange Bowl on New Year's Day, 1963.

extra point gave Tech a 7-0 lead at intermission.

The Crimson Tide gained control of the contest in the second half but again it was Tech mistakes that led to scoring. With only minutes remaining in the game, a severe rush was applied to punter Lothridge by Bill Battle and Richard Williamson. Lothridge's knee touched the ground at his own 9-yard line before he could get the punt away and Alabama had the ball.

Cotton Clark burst 7 yards for the touchdown and it was 7-6. There was a little more than 2 minutes remaining and Bryant figured it was his last scoring opportunity so he ordered a 2-point conversion attempt. Jack Hurlburt carried into the line but was stopped inches short of the goal.

Surprisingly, however, the Tide had one opportunity left. An onsides kickoff was recovered by Alabama's Benny Nelson, and Namath passed and ran to the Georgia

1964 Sugar Bowl—Alabama's Tim Davis (40) kicks one of four field goals to beat Mississippi, 12-7.

Tech 14 for a first down. There were 66 seconds left and Namath dropped back to pass. He rifled the ball toward the goal line but Georgia Tech's Don Toner stepped in to intercept. It was Tech's fifth interception of the day and the Yellow Jackets and Grant Field went wild. Dodd later called it "the greatest Georgia Tech victory."

Alabama recovered the next week to bomb Auburn 33-0 and accepted a bid to the Orange Bowl to be matched against Oklahoma, which had lost only to Notre Dame 13-7 and Texas 9-7. The Sooners were averaging 26.7 points per game.

1963: ALABAMA 17, OKLAHOMA 0

This was the day the nation discovered Joe Namath and, incidentally, found how swift and devastating

Alabama's lines can be. Jordan was remarkable both blocking and tackling and he had help from people such as Jimmy Sharpe, Bill Battle, Butch Wilson, Ed Versprille, Dan Kearley, Frankie McClendon, Charley Pell and Jimmy Wilson.

President John F. Kennedy, a friend of Oklahoma Coach Bud Wilkinson, did the coin flipping prior to the game and sat on the Oklahoma side of the Orange Bowl but it didn't help. The Sooners lost the coin toss, and in less than eight minutes, Namath fired a 25-yard touchdown pass to right end Williamson.

In the second period Namath was at it again. He passed 20 yards to Williamson from the Sooner 34. Versprille lost a yard but Clark dashed around left end for the touchdown and a 14-0 halftime lead. Tim Davis kicked a 9-yard field goal in the third quarter and the Tide had another victory. For the fifteen seniors on the team it finished the best three years in Alabama history—29 victories, two losses, and two ties.

"Walking around the dressing room shaking hands with them after their last game it was all I could do to keep from completely choking up. You just love them, that's all," Bryant said afterward.

Losses to Florida (10-6) and Auburn (10-8) marked 1963 as the first season since 1959 that Alabama had known two defeats in one season. But the Sugar Bowl beckoned anyway and the Tide accepted the challenge against undefeated Southeastern Conference Champion Mississippi, rated a two-touchdown favorite.

1964: ALABAMA 12, MISSISSIPPI 7

But there were some unusual happenings before the game was played. First, on December 9, Bryant suspended Namath for the final game against Miami December 14 and the Sugar Bowl. Bryant said only that Namath had

1964 Sugar Bowl—Alabama players carry Bear Bryant off the field after beating Ole Miss, 12-7.

broken training rules, refusing to specify which rules were violated.

That left the quarterbacking duties to Steve Sloan, who had not thrown a pass all season.

It snowed New Year's Eve in New Orleans and the following afternoon neophyte Sloan led the Crimson Tide to victory, setting up four field goals by Tim Davis of 48, 46, 31 and 22 yards, establishing a bowl record for both number and longest (48).

Alabama recovered six of eleven Ole Miss fumbles and intercepted three passes to survive the imbalance in the statistics that showed the losers piling up 248 yards to 194 for the Tide. The Alabama defense halted the Rebels four times in the final quarter near the goal line at the 2, 9, and 28. Perry Lee Dunn passed 5 yards to Larry Smith for

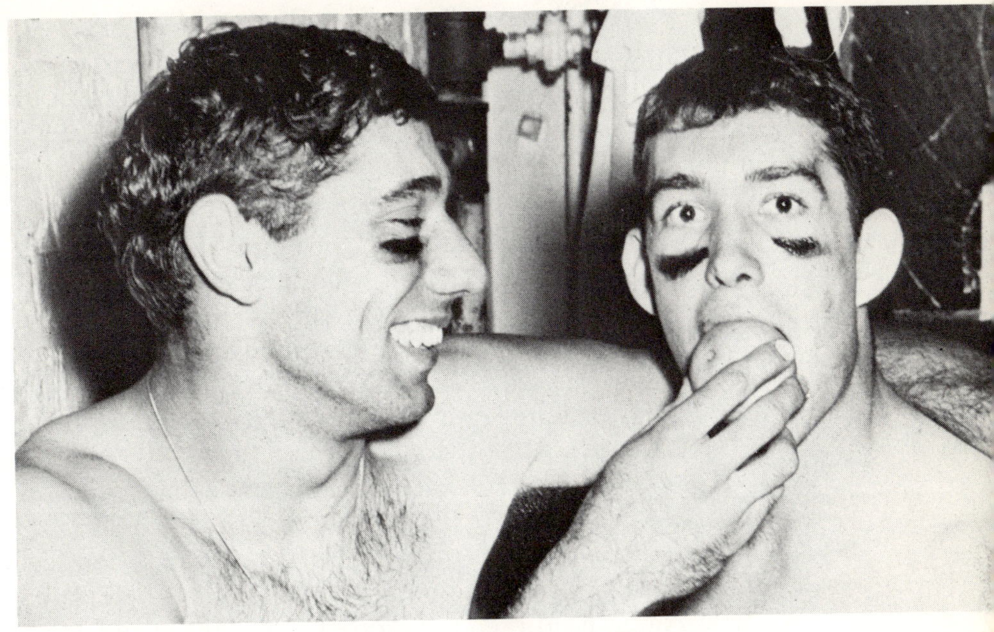

Joe Namath clowns with his understudy, Steve Sloan, after Alabama defeated Auburn, 21-14, to complete an undefeated regular season in 1964.

Mississippi's only touchdown in the frantic final period. It ended Mississippi's nineteen-game unbeaten streak.

The rest of 1964 was extremely profitable, if hectic, for Alabama. Namath, bothered by recurrent knee injuries, missed much of the season and Bryant fretted about his defense, which gave up 50 points in the last five games. Still the Crimson Tide won everything in sight, the Southeastern Conference title, ten consecutive games, and the National Championship, which then was voted on regular season play only.

Sloan stepped in at quarterback to spell the ailing Namath and the Tide escaped a last-second scare against Auburn to complete its second perfect season in four years.

1964: ALABAMA 21, AUBURN 14

Halfback Ray Ogden raced 107 yards with the second half kickoff to spark the Tide's comeback against the Tigers. Steve Bowman had recovered an Auburn fumble in the end zone in the first quarter to give the Tide a brief 6-0 lead.

The conversion, however, failed and Auburn took the lead 7-6 in the second period when Tucker Frederickson scored on a three-yard plunge and the kick was made. Ogden's run, however, Sloan's 2-point conversion, and Joe Namath's 23-yard scoring pass to Ray Perkins in the fourth quarter built up a 21-7 lead. That was enough to survive Auburn's late score.

The Tide figured that Namath would have time to regain his health before the Orange Bowl date with Texas, the defending national champion of 1963, which had lost only to Arkansas by one point. But three days before the battle, Namath suffered a reinjury of his right knee during practice while handing off to a halfback.

1965: TEXAS 21, ALABAMA 17

There were 23 seconds left in the first quarter when Texas' Ernie Koy took a pitchout, cut inside, and scampered 79 yards for a touchdown, setting an Orange Bowl record. Early in the second period, after a 'Bama drive led by Sloan faltered, quarterback Jim Hudson of Texas hurled a 69-yard scoring bomb to George Sauer.

That's when Namath came off the bench, against the wishes of Bryant. He led the Tide immediately on an 87-yard touchdown march in which his passes accounted for 81 yards, cutting the deficit to 14-7. The last 7 yards were covered on a toss to sophomore Wayne Trimble.

Then misfortune struck the Tide late in the first half. Creed Gilmer blocked a Texas field goal but the ball bounced forward far enough to register a first down when the Longhorns recovered. A pass interference penalty

Alabama backfield, 1964.
From left: Joe Namath, Ray Ogden, Steve Bowman, Larry Wall.

gave Texas another first down at the Tide 13 and three plays later Koy circled right end for the final yard and a 21-7 intermission lead.

Namath started the second half and rapidly had Alabama in the Texas end zone again on four passes covering 57 yards. The last went to Perkins for 20 yards and it was 21-14.

Early in the final quarter Alabama's Jim Fuller intercepted a Marv Kristynik pass at the Texas 34 and when Namath got two fast first downs with his passing it appeared the Crimson Tide had finally assumed command. From the 6-yard line, fullback Steve Bowman carried three times, moving the ball to the 1 on fourth down. Namath, despite his gimpy knee, tried to sneak in and was buried by Texans Lammons, Doerr, Nobis, Goad, Hensley, and Sauer.

Pete Lammons intercepted a Namath pass at his 32 in the final minutes to preserve the Texas upset of the national champs.

Coach Darrell Royal said he was happy he would never have to face Namath again. "He is one of the greatest quarterbacks I've ever seen," Royal said. "What makes him so great is the ability to find that spot. He is fantastic in anticipating pass routes and he threads that ball in there."

One survey five years later ranked the Texas-Alabama battle as one of the 40 best college games ever played.

The 1965 season was one of the zaniest ever and the circumstances leading to the Tide's second consecutive national title were almost fictional. It began with a thrill in the opening game but the results suggested anything but another championship season for Alabama.

1965: GEORGIA 18, ALABAMA 17

There was a national audience waiting to see what Bryant had concocted from what remained of his defending champions who were minus Namath, many of his cohorts, and had a revamped defense.

Georgia Coach Vince Dooley, however, was the man with the surprise. A field goal by Bobby Etter and a 55-yard pass interception return by All-American defensive back George Patton had the Bulldogs up 10-0 by halftime.

But Sloan rallied the Tide with his passing and Bowman handled the ground attack in the second half and in a little more than 20 minutes Alabama had a 17-10 lead.

With just a few minutes left Georgia had the ball on its own 27-yard line and their case appeared hopeless. Georgia quarterback Kirby Moore passed to end Pat Hodgson, who was hit hard and began heading for the turf. He flipped the ball back to halfback Bob Taylor who raced for a touchdown completing the 73-yard play.

Alabama protested that Hodgson was on his knees when he made the lateral and thus the play should have been halted there. A picture of the play seemed to show that Hodgson was on his knees while still holding the ball.

A conference official, however, ruled two days later that the play was legal stating: "All three officials saw Hodgson's knees were on the ground but they agreed he did not have the ball long enough to rule he had control of it. If he had dropped it, it would have been ruled an incomplete pass."

Still Georgia trailed 17-16 but Moore passed for a 2-point play to Hodgson. Alabama was beaten. It would not lose again, however, until more than two years later when Tennessee prevailed 24-13 on October 21, 1967.

Although Georgia was the last loss of the year, it didn't mean 1965 would be devoid of thrills. The Tide came back again and again, scratching out a 7-7 tie with Tennessee, edging Mississippi State 10-7 and barely clipping Ole Miss in a tingler 17-16. It was a season to test Bryant's nerves and even the S.E.C. title, the second of three in a row, wasn't decided until the final game when Sloan passed for three touchdowns and the defense intercepted seven passes to beat Auburn 30-3.

Any hope for a national title remained just an hallucination. There were three other teams with perfect records—Michigan State, Arkansas, and Nebraska—ahead of the Crimson Tide in the polls. Fortunately for the Tide, however, the Associated Press was now waiting until after the bowl game results to take the final vote on the champion.

Alabama was scheduled for a night engagement in the Orange Bowl against Nebraska. But before they had even taken the field a remarkable series of events took place. First, in the Cotton Bowl, second-ranked Arkansas lost to Louisiana State 14-7. Three hours later top-rated Michigan State was upset by U.C.L.A. 14-12, and suddenly the Crimson Tide had a chance to be No. 1 again.

1966: ALABAMA 39, NEBRASKA 28

Nebraska outweighed the Tide an average of almost 30 pounds per man but the added beef wasn't necessarily an asset against the lightning-quick Tide. Sloan, the 185-pound quarterback, bombarded the Cornhuskers with 20 completions in 28 attempts for 296 yards, all Orange Bowl records. Ray Perkins did most of the catching while Leslie Kelley and Bowman penetrated the Nebraska defense and by halftime the Tide had piled up a 24-7 lead.

Tom Somerville started the action by recovering a Nebraska fumble at the Alabama 39. Sloan moved quickly and a 21-yard pass to Perkins completed a seven-play drive. Kelley slashed in for a score then Perkins grabbed an 11-yard Sloan touchdown aerial. Bowman scored twice in the second half and the Tide was able to survive the late Husker rally.

Bryant glowed:

"Those little ole skinny things have big hearts. I don't know what it takes to be No. 1 but I guess with everybody getting beat today, we're it."

Bryant was correct this time. Three days later the Tide was voted the champs. But the following season Bryant was asking the same question with different results from the polls.

His 1966 edition rolled through 10 opponents unbeaten and untied, and by November 26 had the only perfect record in college football but ranked only third behind Notre Dame and Michigan State who had played each other to a 10-10 deadlock in what was called the game of the decade. Alabama's only close call had been an 11-10 victory over Tennessee which required an 11-point rally in the fourth quarter.

After quarterback Kenny Stabler had thrown three

Ray Perkins,
All-American end, 1966.

touchdown passes to lead a 34-0 blanking of Southern Mississippi for the Tide's ninth win of the season, Bryant asked:

"I just wish the players and I knew what the people who vote wanted. We'd do it. Back in January we started preparing to win it again this year. Then in September we were voted No. 1 in the pre-season poll and we thought that meant they expected us to win. Well, we've been winning," Bryant said. "It was said that no team had ever beaten Tennessee, Mississippi, and Louisiana State in the same year. Well, our players did it. It's also been said that the Southeastern Conference is a tough conference and our players lead it in offense and defense.

"If the voters want something besides winning, we'll try triple reverses, forward laterals, lateral forwards, dipsy-doodles, or even run a quarterback sneak on third and 9. Our players have done everything we've asked."

The Tide completed the regular season the following week with a 31-0 swamping of Auburn and had shut out six of ten opponents, yielding a total of 37 points. They had averaged using 53 players a game. Still they were third.

1967: ALABAMA 34, NEBRASKA 7

As if angry over their rating, the Tide dominated Nebraska from the opening play when Kenny (Snake) Stabler whipped a 45-yard left-handed strike to Perkins that set up Kelley's 1-yard scoring plunge and a 17-point first quarter.

On Alabama's second possession Stabler threw for 9 and then 42 yards, 6 again and, then sprinted 14 yards for the score. A Steve Davis field goal and a 71-yard scoring march in ten plays gave the Tide a 24-0 halftime lead. Stabler and Perkins combined on a 45-yard scoring bomb, and the statistics showed Stabler connecting on 12 of 17 for 218 yards and gaining 40 yards on the ground.

"This is the greatest college football team I've ever seen or ever been associated with," Bryant said afterward.

Nebraska Coach Bob Devaney wasn't disputing Bryant.

"Alabama is several touchdowns stronger than the team that beat us a year ago," Devaney said. "Stabler was just too quick for the people we had chasing him."

But Notre Dame was voted No. 1.

There would be no championships—either national or conference—the remainder of the 1960s, and although the bowl invitations continued coming, the victories did not accompany them. In fact, through 1973, the Crimson Tide was winless in seven consecutive bowls including one tie.

That didn't mean there weren't some scintillating games. One of the most memorable was the opening contest of 1967 when Florida State came from behind to earn a 37-37 tie before a shocked gathering at Legion Field.

A month later the nation's longest undefeated streak ended at 25 games when Tennessee's third-string quarterback Bubba Wyche, switched to a surprise starting role, led the Vols to a 24-13 upset. The game was tied 7-7 in the third period when the Vols' Steve Delong scored on an 11-yard pass from Walter Chadwick. Karl Kresmer added a 47-yard field goal in the third period before the Tide came back to cut the lead to 17-13 early in the fourth quarter.

But defensive back Albert Dorsey intercepted a Stabler pass, returned it 31 yards for the clinching score and the Vols won to start a Tennessee string of four consecutive victories at the Tide's expense.

The bowl losses began in the Cotton Bowl on January 1, 1968, when Texas A.&M., coached by former Bryant pupil Gene Stallings, 32, held off repeated Alabama thrusts in the fourth period and went home clinging to a tense 20-16 victory.

One of the most painful Alabama defeats came a year later in the Gator Bowl when the Missouri Tigers demolished the Tide with a fourth-quarter explosion of three touchdowns, 35-10. It was the worst beating any of Bryant's Alabama teams had ever absorbed. Alabama had a minus 45 yards rushing and a total offense of just 23 yards compared with 402 yards on the ground for the Tigers, who got three short touchdown plunges from Terry McMillan.

The Big Eight wasn't through with the Tide. In the Liberty Bowl, December 13, 1968, Colorado rolled to a 17-point lead early and held a 31-19 advantage at halftime. Alabama soared ahead in the third quarter 33-31 behind the play of quarterback Neb Hayden and Johnny Musso who combined on the go-ahead touchdown.

But Colorado marched 53 yards in 12 plays and Bob Anderson scored the second of his three touchdowns from the two, restoring the Buffs to a 38-33 lead. A safety and a touchdown by Anderson in the final 45 seconds gave Colorado a 47-33 victory and the greatest decade of football came to an inappropriate conclusion.

17

The Wishbone

By Bear Bryant's yardstick the 1970s began as a disaster. The Crimson Tide was embarrassed on its own turf in Legion Field in the opening game of 1970 by Southern Cal, which waltzed to a 42-21 triumph. Three weeks later against Ole Miss the contest was billed as a rematch of the 1969 passing duel between the Rebels' Archie Manning and Alabama's Scott Hunter. Manning had gained 540 yards in the '69 meeting, Hunter had passed for 300 and the Tide won 33-32 in one of the most sensational games in the series.

Now the two quarterbacks were supposed to clash again. But on the eve of the contest Hunter was sidelined with a shoulder separation and the Crimson Tide seemed to go with him.

Manning accounted for five touchdowns despite playing with a pulled leg muscle. Substitute Alabama quarterback Neb Hayden made a game of it for awhile, throwing three touchdown passes himself and the Tide trimmed a

Alabama's Johnny Musso tries to evade two Auburn defenders in 1971 game in Birmingham. Alabama won, 31-7.

26-3 halftime deficit down to 26-17. Then Manning went to work and the Rebels romped away with a 48-23 victory.

As if that wasn't humiliation enough, two weeks later Tennessee administered the first shutout to Alabama 24-0 since the 1959 Liberty Bowl defeat at the hands of Penn State, 7-0.

Fumed Bryant afterward:

"As an alumnus I'm getting disguted with the coaching. We've lost practically every big game we've had the last two years. It's the same old story. We've been out-coached."

Somehow Bryant managed to salvage the rest of the year and wangle another bowl invitation with a 6-5 record despite losses to L.S.U. and Auburn.

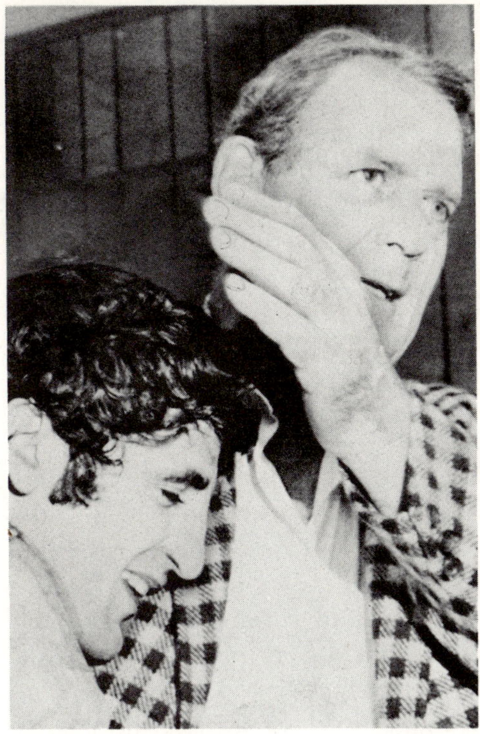

Bear Bryant pats head of Johnny Musso after 31-7 victory over Auburn gave the Tide the S.E.C. championship for 1971.

The Auburn loss was particularly painful because the Tide blew a 17-point first-quarter lead and the Tigers' passing combination of Pat Sullivan and Terry Beasley carved a 33-28 victory. Hunter had a 54-yard touchdown pass to George Ranager and Johnny Musso became the first running back in Alabama's long history to gain over 1,000 yards in a season, but it was small consolation.

There was still a stop in the Bluebonnet Bowl and that left more bitter memories. Oklahoma's Sooners marched 61 yards in the final minutes, setting up a 42-yard field goal by Bruce Derr with 56 seconds remaining. That earned the Sooners a 24-24 tie with 'Bama and Bryant felt changes had to be made.

1971: ALABAMA 17, SOUTHERN CALIFORNIA 10

Bryant had suffered through his first season that contained five setbacks using the pro-style formation with the drop-back passer, Hunter. At the same time Coach Darrell Royal at Texas had his Longhorns running over everybody with the innovative Wishbone formation that had a baffling array of options. Thus in the spring of 1971 Bryant set out to learn all he could about the Wishbone, meeting twice with Royal and studying films of Texas' games. Bryant figured that his personnel didn't fit the pro set formations and the Wishbone might be more adaptable. He thought it was worth the gamble.

The first game of '71 would be a severe test for the new formation. The Crimson Tide had to visit the Southern California Trojans in Los Angeles with the memory of what the Trojans had done to them in Birmingham the previous September. Oddsmakers figured Southern Cal was a 10-point to 2-touchdown favorite. What they had not figured on was how perfectly the Wishbone fitted the Crimson Tide.

And the man who made it go was Musso, the Italian Stallion, who burst loose on runs of 8 and 13 yards for touchdowns. Bill Davis found the range with a 37-yard field goal and the Crimson Tide rolled to a 17-0 lead. The defense, led by All-Americans Robin Parkhouse at end and Tom Surlas at linebacker, yielded just 10 points the rest of the night to the powerful Trojan offense and Bryant was back in business with his 200th victory, 17-10.

1972: NEBRASKA 38, ALABAMA 6

Alabama marched on to an 11-0 regular season record, started another string of Southeastern Conference championships and it would have been a wonderful season if the bowl miseries hadn't struck again.

It was a perfect setting, No. 1 ranked Nebraska and No. 2 rated Alabama on New Year's night in the Orange

Bowl. It was the game that was imperfect, from the view of Alabama followers.

The Cornhuskers struck early on Alabama mistakes, and Johnny Rodgers broke for a dazzling 77-yard touchdown on a punt return. Nebraska had nine first downs before the Tide could manage two and had 28 points on the board in less than 22 minutes. Only twice in the first half did Alabama get as far as the Nebraska 40-yard line. Quarterback Jerry Tagge of the Cornhuskers completed 11 of 19 passes for 159 yards, scored a touchdown and sent Jeff Kinney off on gains that netted 99 yards in 20 carries. Nebraska's reserves played most of the second half and Alabama was thoroughly beaten 38-6. Coach Bob Devaney, after a dunking in the showers, confirmed that "This was the biggest win of my career."

Said Bryant: "They toyed with us most of the time. They were one of the greats, if not the greatest, I have ever seen."

Undaunted, Bryant set out with the Wishbone again in 1972 and the victories began coming. Until the final game of the season the only close call for the Crimson Tide came from the typically tough Volunteers of Tennessee.

The Vols led 10-3 late in the fourth quarter but in the space of 36 seconds the Tide got two touchdowns on a 2-yard run by Wilbur Jackson and a 22-yard sprint by quarterback Terry Davis for a 17-10 victory.

A perfect season loomed in the final game against Auburn. The Tide led 16-0 entering the final period and when Auburn's Gardner Jett kicked a 42-yard field goal no one seemed concerned because Alabama had dominated the game.

On Alabama's next possession, Bill Newton and Ken Bernich led a rush on Alabama punter Greg Gantt and managed to block the kick. The ball bounced into the arms of David Langer who raced 25 yards for a

Alabama backfield, 1971.
From left: Terry Davis, Johnny Musso, Steve Bisceglia, Joe LaBue.

touchdown. Jett's extra point cut the lead to 16-10 and now there was some restlessness.

Alabama took the ensuing kickoff and moved to the 43 before Gantt was called on to punt again. Once again Auburn, faking a ten-man pass rush, flooded one side and slipped the linebacker through. Newton again blocked the punt, again Langer broke through the same hole, got the same kind of bounce and took the ball 20 yards for the tying touchdown. Jett's kick gave Auburn a 17-16 upset and ruined a perfect season and the hopes for another national title.

1973: TEXAS 17, ALABAMA 13

A duel of Wishbone offenses was left for the Tide, which now had slipped to fourth in the rankings. Seventh-ranked Texas was the opposition and again the Tide jumped to a 10-0 first quarter lead only to falter. A 13-3 halftime advantage disappeared. Texas' Alan Lowry, a defensive back converted to quarterback, and fullback Roosevelt Leaks led drives of 59 yards in the third period and 80 yards in the fourth quarter that gave the Longhorns a 17-13 lead with 4:22 remaining. Lowry scored the touchdowns on runs of 3 and 34 yards while Leaks gained 120 yards inside.

Texas used two interceptions and a last-ditch stand to survive and hand Bryant another bowl defeat.

The 1973 season found Alabama again bidding for the highest honors in collegiate football even though Bryant had to do some reshuffling of talent.

As Bryant later reflected just before the Sugar Bowl game on New Year's Eve against Notre Dame for the national title:

"At the start of the season we didn't know who our regular offensive guards would be; the same at center. On defense we had to make replacements for an All-American end (John Mitchell) and several in the secondary. Fortunately, the schedule worked to our advantage. We got some early leads and were able to play a lot of men to find out what we really had. The men worked and yes, by mid-season, I did say this might be my best Alabama team ever. It could work out that way."

1973: ALABAMA 42, TENNESSEE 21

Bryant's Wishbone was devastating. It was on the field so much in 1973 the defense had less than its usual amount of playing time. And to supplement the offense Bryant came up with three speedy, hard-striking units, one almost as good as the other. Wilbur Jackson was the primary runner and the three offensive squads together averaged 366 yards rushing. Against Virginia Tech they piled up a record 833 yards total offense including 748 on the ground. Gary Rutledge and Richard Todd alternated at quarterback and both had success throwing when Bryant felt it was needed.

An example of passing power came against Tennessee in the sixth game of the season. On the first play of the game, Rutledge unleashed an 80-yard scoring bomb to Wayne Wheeler and the Tide jumped to a quick 14-0 lead. But this was also the day the Tide got its biggest test. By the start of the fourth quarter Tennessee, behind slippery little quarterback Conredge Holloway's two long touchdown passes and 6-yard scoring run, had pulled into a 21-21 tie.

But within a span of a few minutes of the fourth period the explosive Tide had registered 21 points to stop any thought of an upset. Robin Cary started it with a 64-yard touchdown dash on a punt return. Jackson broke loose almost immediately thereafter on an 80-yard scoring scamper, and fullback Paul Spivey completed the rally with a 3-yard touchdown run.

Alabama's depth had worn down Tennessee as it had done to all other opponents in its path. The 1973 squad had scored a record 454 points and permitted only 89, won eleven consecutive regular season games and marched into the 40th Sugar Bowl in New Orleans ranked No. 1 in the country with a triumph over undefeated Notre Dame needed to prove it.

1973: NOTRE DAME 24, ALABAMA 23

"This was a great night for the Irish. It was the greatest day or night in the history of Notre Dame's Fighting Irish. It was one of the greatest games ever played in college football," wrote one wildly enthusiastic Notre Dame supporter.

Indeed, it was a sensational game and Bear Bryant lamented afterward that his team hadn't lost. "Time just ran out on us," Bryant said.

Alabama's Wilbur Jackson (80) breaks through Tennessee line for a touchdown from the 4-yard line in first-quarter action, 1973.

The lead changed hands six times after Notre Dame grabbed a quick 6-0 advantage. Finally it came down to the final 4 minutes and 12 seconds and Notre Dame's Bob Thomas was asked to kick a 19-yard field goal which gave the Irish a 24-23 lead. Three minutes remained when Alabama's Greg Gantt boomed a 69-yard punt that was downed on the Notre Dame one. Officials called Notre Dame for roughing the punter.

With Notre Dame backed up to its one, Bryant declined the penalty.

"The penalty wouldn't have given Alabama a first down and I had no doubt he'd decline it," said Notre Dame Coach Ara Parseghian. "It's actually like Bryant's on offense and we're on defense. If we have to punt, even a goal.''

There were only two minutes left when Parseghian faced a decision of his own. It was third down, 8 and the ball was on the Notre Dame 3-yard line. It seemed almost certain Notre Dame would have to punt and Alabama would have plenty of time to maneuver for the winning field goal.

But Parseghian gambled and called for a pass. Quarterback Tom Clements executed the gamble. Clements stood cooly in the end zone and fired a 35-yard strike to tight end Robin Weber and time ran out on Alabama.

"That play won it for us," Parseghian said. "It meant everything in the world. It was a win-or-punt situation."

Bryant agreed:

"That pass beat us. If we get the ball back we're going to win the game. When we had them backed up to the 1-yard line, if I'd been a betting man I'd have bet you anything we were going to win . . . .There are a lot of so-called turning points in this kind of game. We didn't throw enough on first downs. That's one thing. And our hard rush makes us vulnerable to misdirection plays . . . .Sure Notre Dame is a great team. But I wouldn't mind playing them again tomorrow. In fact, I'd like it."

There was little doubt that Alabama would get another chance. Being in a championship game is just something it rarely misses. It's a tradition that has been earned over many years at Tuscaloosa.

Appendix:
Alabama Records

Alabama Coaches and Records

Year	Coach	Captain	Record	Pts.	Opp.
1892	E. B. Beaumont (Penn)	W. G. Little	2-2-0	96	37
1893	Eli Abbott (Penn)	G. H. Kyzer	0-4-0	24	74
1894	Eli Abbott	S. B. Slone	3-1-0	60	16
1895	Eli Abbott	H. M. Bankhead	0-4-0	12	112
1896	Otto Wagonhurst (Penn)	S. B. Slone	2-1-0	56	10
1897	Allen McCants (Alabama)	Frank S. White, Jr	1-0-0	6	0
1898	No Team	T. G. Burk—Elected	No Team		
1899	W. A. Hartin (Virginia)	T. W. Wert	3-1-0	39	31
1900	M. Griffin	W. E. Drennen	2-3-0	52	100
1901	M. H. Harvey (Auburn)	W. E. Drennen	2-1-2	92	23
1902	Eli Abbott, J. O. Heyworth	J. R. Forman	4-4-0	191	49
1903	W. B. Blount (Yale)	W. S. Wyatt	3-4-0	60	114
1904	W. B. Blount	W. S. Wyatt	7-3-0	100	62
1905	Jack Leavenworth (Yale)	B. A. Burks	6-4-0	178	113
1906	J. W. H. Pollard (Dartmouth)	Washington Moody	5-1-0	97	82
1907	J. W. H. Pollard	Emile Hannon	5-1-2	70	64
1908	J. W. H. Pollard	Henry Burks	6-1-1	107	31
1909	J. W. H. Pollard	Derrill Pratt	5-1-2	68	17
1910	Guy S. Lowman (Springfield)	O. G. Gresham	4-4-0	65	107
1911	D. V. Graves (Missouri)	R. H. Bumgardner	5-2-2	153	31
1912	D. V. Graves	Farley W. Moody	5-3-1	156	55
1913	D. V. Graves	C. H. Van de Graaff	5-3-0	188	40
1914	D. V. Graves	C. A. "Tubby" Long	5-4-0	211	64

Year	Coach	Captain	Record		
1915	Thomas Kelly (Chicago)	William L. Harsh	6-2-0	250	51
1916	Thomas Kelly	Lowndes Morton	6-3-0	156	62
1917	Thomas Kelly	Jack Hovater	5-2-1	169	29
1918	No Team	Dan Boone—Elected	No Team		
1919	Xen C. Scott (Western Reserve)	Isaac J. Rogers	8-1-0	280	22
1920	Xen C. Scott	Sid Johnston	10-1-0	377	35
1921	Xen C. Scott	Al Clemens	5-4-2	241	104
1922	Xen C. Scott	Ernest E. Cooper	6-3-1	300	81
1923	Wallace Wade (Brown)	Al Clemens	7-2-1	222	50
1924	Wallace Wade	A. T. S. Hubert	8-1-0	290	24
1925	Wallace Wade	Bruce Jones	10-0-0	297	26
1926	Wallace Wade	Emile "Red" Barnes	9-0-1	249	27
1927	Wallace Wade	Freddie Pickhard	5-4-1	154	73
1928	Wallace Wade	Earle Smith	6-3-0	187	75
1929	Wallace Wade	Billy Hicks	6-3-0	196	58
1930	Wallace Wade	Charles B. Clement	10-0-0	271	13
1931	Frank W. Thomas (Notre Dame)	Joe Sharpe	9-1-0	370	57
1932	Frank W. Thomas	John Cain	8-2-0	200	51
1933	Frank W. Thomas	Foy Leach	7-1-1	130	17
1934	Frank W. Thomas	Bill Lee	10-0-0	316	45
1935	Frank W. Thomas	James Walker	6-2-1	185	55
1936	Frank W. Thomas	Jas. "Bubber" Nisbet	8-0-1	168	35
1937	Frank W. Thomas	Leroy Monsky	9-1-0	225	33
1938	Frank W. Thomas	Lew Bostick	7-1-1	149	40
1939	Frank W. Thomas	Carey Cox	5-3-1	101	53
1940	Frank W. Thomas	Harold Newman	7-2-0	166	80
1941	Frank W. Thomas	John Wyhonic	9-2-0	263	85
1942	Frank W. Thomas	Joe Domnanovich	8-3-0	246	97

Year	Coach	Captain	Record	Pts.	Opp.
1943	No Team	No Team		No Team	
1944	Frank W. Thomas	Game Captains	5-2-2	272	83
1945	Frank W. Thomas	Game Captains	10-0-0	430	80
1946	Frank W. Thomas	Game Captains	7-4-0	186	110
1947	H. D. Drew (Bates)	John Wozniak	8-3-0	210	101
1948	H. D. Drew	Ray Richeson	6-4-1	228	170
1949	H. D. Drew	Doug Lockridge	6-3-1	227	130
1950	H. D. Drew	Mike Mizerany	9-2-0	328	107
1951	H. D. Drew	Jack Brown	5-6-0	263	188
1952	H. D. Drew	Bobby Wilson	10-2-0	325	139
1953	H. D. Drew	Bud Willis	6-3-3	178	152
1954	H. D. Drew	Sid Youngleman	4-5-2	123	104
1955	J. B. Whitworth (Alabama)	Nick Germanos	0-10-0	48	255
1956	J. B. Whitworth	Jim Cunningham-Wes Thompson	2-7-1	85	208
1957	J. B. Whitworth	Jim Loftis-Clay Walls	2-7-1	69	173
1958	Paul W. Bryant (Alabama)	Dave Sington-Bobby Smith	5-4-1	106	75
1959	Paul W. Bryant	Marlin Dyess-Jim Blevins	7-2-2	95	59
1960	Paul W. Bryant	Leon Fuller-Bobby Boylston	8-1-2	183	56

Year	Coach	Captain(s)	Record	Points For	Points Against
1961	Paul W. Bryant	Pat Trammell-Billy Neighbors	11-0-0	297	25
1962	Paul W. Bryant	Lee Roy Jordan-Jimmy Sharpe	10-1-0	289	39
1963	Paul W. Bryant	Benny Nelson-Steve Allen	9-2-0	227	105
1964	Paul W. Bryant	Joe Namath-Ray Ogden	10-1-0	250	88
1965	Paul W. Bryant	Steve Sloan-Paul Crane	9-1-1	256	107
1966	Paul W. Bryant	Ray Perkins-Richard Cole	11-0-0	301	44
1967	Paul W. Bryant	Ken Stabler-Bobby Johns	8-2-1	198	131
1968	Paul W. Bryant	Mike Hall-Donnie Sutton	8-3-0	184	139
1969	Paul W. Bryant	Danny Ford-Alvin Samples	6-5-0	314	268
1970	Paul W. Bryant	Danny Gilbert-Dave Brungard	6-5-1	334	264
1971	Paul W. Bryant	Johnny Musso-Robin Parkhouse	11-1-0	368	122
1972	Paul W. Bryant	Terry Davis-John Mitchell	10-2-0	406	150
1973	Paul W. Bryant	(to be elected)	11-1-0	477	113

Total Record **500-188-41**

Alabama's All-Americans

1973—Woodrow Lowe, L.B.
Wayne Wheeler, O.E.
Buddy Brown, O.T.
1972—John Hannah, guard (O)
John Mitchell, end (D)
Jim Krapf, center (O)
1971—Johnny Musso,
halfback (O)
John Hannah, guard (O)
Tom Surlas,
linebacker (D)
Robin Parkhouse, end
(D)
1970—Johnny Musso,
tailback (O)
1969—Alvin Samples, guard (O)
1968—Mike Hall, linebacker (D)
Sam Gellerstedt,
guard (D)
1967—Dennis Homan,
split end (O)
Bobby Johns,
halfback (D)
Kenny Stabler,
quarterback (O)

1966—Richard Cole, tackle (D)
Ray Perkins, end (O)
Cecil Dowdy, tackle (O)
Bobby Johns,
halfback (D)
1965—Paul Crane, center
Steve Sloan, quarterback
1964—Wayne Freeman, guard
Dan Kearley, tackle
David Ray, halfback
Joe Namath, quarterback
1962—Lee Roy Jordan, center
1961—Billy Neighbors, tackle
Pat Trammell,
quarterback
Lee Roy Jordan, center
1950—Ed Salem, halfback
1945—Harry Gilmer, halfback
Vaughn Mancha, center
1942—Don Whitmire, tackle
Joe Domnanovich, center

1941—Holt Rast, end
1939—Carey Cox, center
1937—James Ryba, tackle
Leroy Monsky, guard
Joe Kilgrow, halfback
1936—Arthur "Tarzan"
White, guard
1935—Riley Smith, quarterback
1934—Millard "Dixie"
Howell, halfback
Don Hutson, end
Bill Lee, tackle
1933—Tom Hupke, guard
1931—Johnny Cain, fullback
1930—Fred Sington, tackle
1930—John Suther, halfback
1929—Tony Holm, fullback
1926—Hoyt "Wu" Winslett, end
1925—A. T. S. "Pooley"
Hubert, quarterback
1915—W. T. "Bully" Van-
deGraaff, tackle